# ALL WORK, NO PAY

# ALL WORK, NO PAY

## FINDING AN INTERNSHIP,
Building Your **Resume,**
Making **Connections,** and
Gaining **Job Experience**

## LAUREN BERGER
The Intern Queen

**TEN SPEED PRESS**
Berkeley

Published in the United States by Ten Speed Press, an imprint of the
Crown Publishing Group, a division of Random House, Inc., New York.
www.crownpublishing.com
www.tenspeed.com

Ten Speed Press and the Ten Speed Press colophon are registered trademarks
of Random House, Inc.

Library of Congress Cataloging-in-Publication Data
Berger, Lauren.
    All work, no pay : finding an internship, building your resume, making
connections, and gaining job experience / by Lauren Berger. — 1st ed.
        p. cm.
    Includes bibliographical references and index.
    Summary: "This guide from Intern Queen Lauren Berger shows college
students (and others) how to find and land impressive internships and
get the most out of them, from work experience to networking to resume
building"—Provided by publisher.
    1. Vocational guidance. 2. Internship programs. I. Title.
    HF5381.B3647 2012
    650.14—dc23
                                2011034540

ISBN 978-1-60774-168-8
eISBN 978-1-60774-225-8

Printed in the United States of America

Jacket cover photograph and author photograph, copyright © 2012 by Felicity Murphy
Design by Toni Tajima

10 9 8 7 6 5 4 3 2 1

First Edition

This book is dedicated to my grandma,
Gladys Levine, who always told me
I would be a writer. I love you.

# CONTENTS

# ACKNOWLEDGMENTS

THE MAJORITY OF YOUNG ENTREPRENEURS go through a period when everyone tells them no. I was no exception and definitely went through my own seemingly endless period of rejection after rejection. I have to thank the people who told me no. Unknowingly, they made me prove myself day after day.

## The Parents

My parents, Sherry and Ira Berger, always told me I could do anything and the world was mine. I think they got a little worried when I took that literally and started calling myself the Intern Queen. Mom and Dad, thank you for loving me so much and just letting me be me.

## The Brother

Jonathan, you are hands down the best little guy on the planet—and you aren't so little anymore. You are the president of my fan club, my bodyguard, and, at times, a really good friend. I'm so proud of you.

## The Book Team

To Katie Kotchman, my rock star book agent, who believed this would work from day one and helped me so much along the way. And to Lisa Westmoreland at Ten Speed for all of your guidance and encouragement with my first book project. Thank you so much.

## The Intern Queen Team

To everyone I work with day in and day out—thank you. To my managers, agents, and everyone who has provided any piece of advice along the way—I promise, I'm always listening and I appreciate all of your words of wisdom.

## The Intern Queen Family

To all of my interns over the years, our Intern Queen Campus Ambassadors, and my fans—you are the brightest, most ambitious students out there and will run the world one day. Thank you for building this with me.

## The Friends

I must thank my friends—my rocks. I've been lucky enough to have the kind of friendships that last forever. They exemplify everything I stand for and amaze me every day with their loyalty, love, and continuous support.

# DEAR READER

IN COLLEGE, I FELT LOST. I wanted information on internships but I felt that no one really cared. My friends and I weren't on the same page when it came to the importance of internships. They weren't ready to think about their future. My college's career center didn't have any internship opportunities for students until their junior or senior year. I always wished that *someone* or *something* existed to help me with the process. Where could I go to find internships and learn what to do once I landed one?

And so I taught myself. I created my own methods of finding internships, and, through trial and error, I learned to make the most of them. I finished college having completed multiple internships (fifteen, to be exact) and a friend jokingly referred to me as "the Intern Queen." Near the end of my senior year, I decided that I would use the knowledge gained from my internship experiences to start a business—an online internship destination that would list available opportunities and educate students on how to make the most of them. I would call it www.internqueen.com.

Through my internships, I gained tons of insight about myself, the workplace, and my future. You don't have to do this alone. Let me be the person to guide you on your internship journey. I will provide you with strategies and techniques to find and land great internships—something nobody shared with me.

The state of our economy calls for action. As young people, we must stand up and make things happen. If you are considering this book, or reading this introduction, you should be proud. It's easy to sit around, do nothing, and wait for opportunities to come to you. The most valuable thing I learned from my fifteen internships was that *I* had the ability to make things happen. Obstacles motivate me; rejection motivates me. And I learned how to deal with obstacles and rejection over the course of my internship journey.

Yes, this is a book about internships—how to get an internship, make the most of it, and leverage it for your future. But personally, it means so much more. Ultimately these experiences carried me from where I was to where I wanted to be. They taught me that anything is possible.

Learning and educating yourself through real-world experience will help *you* reach *your* goals. You have two options—to continue reading and take control of your life right now or to put the book back on the shelf. This is your life. You have an opportunity. Let me be a resource for you. Start this book, put my tips to use, and I promise you'll gain valuable experience unlike anything else.

I have squeezed every last bit of myself into this book. My passion for internships, helping young people, and inspiring my generation is like no other. And I promise that my energy is contagious. Enjoy my book—and your upcoming journey.

—Lauren Berger, the Intern Queen

# INTRODUCTION

**AS A COLLEGE FRESHMAN,** I focused on everything except opportunity. My days consisted of binge-studying and social activities. I knew that big career decisions would command my attention in the not-so-distant future, but my focus was elsewhere. I didn't have an answer to the infamous question, "What do you want to be when you grow up?" My parents and teachers would always say, "Lauren, get your act together and figure out what you want to do." But no one provided an action plan that I could follow to move forward. I was always being told I had "lots of potential," but I didn't understand how to turn that into success.

So in 2002, when my mother called and said, "Get an internship," my initial reaction was that I wasn't interested. When I realized my mom wasn't going to let up, I began to seriously consider internship opportunities. Ironically it was my lack of direction that led me into the career center to find more information.

Without rejection, I wouldn't have developed the thick skin that I have today. In fact, my first internship experience began with rejection. I walked into the career center and eagerly announced, "My name is Lauren Berger, and I'd love an internship. My dream job is to work for *Us Weekly* magazine." The two women from the career center stood there and stared at me. They said, "We're sorry, Lauren, but you need to be a junior or senior to intern. There is one company in town called the Zimmerman Agency, but they only accept seniors. We have nothing for you."

Looking back on that experience, I always think, what if I had listened to them? Would I be successful now? The word *no* ignited something inside of me. Somehow I found it challenging and wanted to prove them wrong.

I became determined to land an opportunity and immediately went back to my dorm room to research the Zimmerman Agency and other public relations companies in town.

My first step was to visit their website to learn about their business, clients, and company history. The Zimmerman Agency website displayed no information about internship or career opportunities. I studied the website, making sure I was familiar with the company before I picked up the phone to cold-call.

"Hello, this is Lauren Berger calling. May I speak with your internship coordinator?" The internship coordinator (at the time), Autumn, took my call and requested that I send over a resume and cover letter. I researched how to create these materials online and put my extremely minimal experience into a professional format. My resume screamed "freshman," with my only previous job experience being at the Limited Too and Red Lobster. Luckily I'd participated in several extracurricular activities during high school and had joined some campus groups at Florida State University. I accompanied my resume with a brief cover letter explaining that I was an underclassman but willing to put 150 percent into the position. I emailed my materials to Autumn the day after she requested them. She needed to know this internship was a priority, and I didn't want her to forget our phone conversation. In the body of the email, I wrote the following short note:

> Dear Autumn,
>
> Great speaking with you. Per our conversation, my resume and cover letter are attached. I look forward to speaking with you further.
>
> Best,
> Lauren Berger
> Florida State University
> Phone: 555-555-5555
> Email: lberger@gmail.com

My phone rang the next day, and I was called into the Zimmerman Agency for an interview. They wanted to know if I was available to come into the office the following day. At the beginning of your career, it's important to do everything you can to make yourself available. So I made myself available on the day and at the time they requested. I immediately went out and purchased a plain black business suit that still hangs in my closet. I walked into the interview dressed for success and feeling excited but nervous. I sold myself to Autumn with my passion, energy, and excitement for the position—traits that should never be overlooked or discounted. She hired me on the spot. And just like that, I landed the internship at the Zimmerman Agency. This was the position my career center said I couldn't get until I was a senior. Years later, when I asked Autumn why I was offered the internship she said, "You seemed unstoppable. There was a passion behind your eyes." That still resonates with me today.

I experienced a dramatic change after getting that first internship. At the office, employees fascinated me with their drive, focus, and passion for their work. I felt challenged by the duties I was given and enjoyed learning about the industry, administrative tasks, and new projects.

What surprised me was how this internship distinguished me from my friends. I was no longer able to spend time the way I used to. I started using my free time to not only think about my goals but actually take the necessary steps to achieve them. The internship granted me a sense of direction. I developed a sense of urgency and focus on my career—something I'd never experienced in the past. I—not my parents, not my friends—was in control of my future. I learned that I could still go after what I wanted even when people told me no—and that was a powerful lesson. Through this first internship, my mindset changed—and this is what I call my "click moment." And until I sat down to write this book, I'm not sure I fully understood the integral role that internships played in my life.

This book will take you on a journey through the entire internship process, showing you exactly how an internship can provide the tools to launch and better your career. In the first chapter, I will explain the significance of internships, explore current trends, and provide solutions for students having difficulty fitting internships into their schedule. Remember, the purpose of this book is to show you how to find, land, and make the *most* out of internship opportunities—both paid and unpaid. The first handful of chapters talk about how to find your dream internship, and the last few chapters discuss how to be the best intern ever. Make sure you comb through each section carefully so you don't miss a single piece of advice!

Together we'll go beneath the surface of an internship. I take you past the satirical depictions of interns and guide you directly to the core of internships, where you can transform your college careers. You will finish this book as a focused internship candidate, one who is confident in how to land an internship and who knows how to make the most of the experience. This process is about connecting the dots and identifying opportunities that have a positive long-term effect on your life.

## CHAPTER 1

# The Truth About
# **Internships**

No matter what the common perception of internships might be, they are, inarguably, the most valuable experience for today's college student. And the statistics are there to back it up. In 2010, students with internships on their resume received a greater number of job offers than students without internships. Additionally, students with internship experience received higher salary offers for their first jobs than students without internships.[1] The internship remains the only proven way to provide students with the entry-level job experience, training, and relationships necessary to better prepare them for their career path.

Perhaps the strongest argument for internships stems from those who started as interns and have gone on to be successful. I point you to the likes of Oprah Winfrey, who started as an intern for a local CBS affiliate in Nashville; award-winning journalist Brian Williams, who started as an intern for the Jimmy Carter administration; and fashion designer extraordinaire Betsy Johnson, who started as an intern for *Mademoiselle* magazine. Despite these facts, statistics, and examples, many students across America remain unconvinced and unwilling to consider internships. They don't want to focus their attention on gaining the practical workplace experience usually needed to land a job after college. These students have not experienced their click moment.

I begin my internship presentations at universities by asking students to raise their hands if they've had an internship. Approximately 20 percent raise their hands. Those 20 percent are on the right track. The other 80 percent will be on the right track soon—they just need a bit of encouragement. But why does this happen? What is the disconnect between Gen Y and the concept of internships?

Many call this a generational issue, but I say it's the difference between *knowing* and *doing*. I argue that students do know where they want to go and how they want their life to end up—at least in a general sense. What they do not know is *how* they are going to arrive at their chosen destination. People tend to focus on the end result and overlook the roadmap that shows students how to get from point A to point B. When I was younger, I was constantly asked, "What do you want to be when you grow up?" This question forced me to think about my career goals but failed to show me how I could achieve them. Students understand the importance of landing a job after college. I don't doubt that. However, they often have a lack of guidance for the time in between.

I, too, ask students what they want to be when they grow up. The difference is that I follow up the question by asking *how* they are going to get there. How will you achieve your goal? What internship can you get to further your understanding of a specific industry?

Before we dive into the current internship space and explore internship trends, I want to explain why an internship is a necessary tool for one's future. Below I've outlined five key components of an internship that are crucial to lifelong career success: hands-on education, networking, resume building, gaining references, and pursuit or elimination. To be clear, these five components apply to both paid and unpaid internships.

# HANDS-ON EDUCATION

A hands-on education is something that can't be achieved in the classroom. Your internship not only teaches you what goes on within a company but also provides you with the opportunity to execute and perform these tasks while under the proper mentorship or supervision. As an intern, you handle administrative tasks, sit in on meetings, and develop a clear understanding of *how* executives do *what* they do. You will make mistakes because you are learning. In fact, you are expected to make mistakes. These mistakes help prepare you to excel postcollege, when you are on the company's dime. This knowledge and practice will place you above your competition and ahead of the crowd for job interviews. Mary Mahoney, assistant director of Career Services at the University of Tennessee says, "If you were an employer, who would you rather hire: the student with no previous experience or the student who's had intense training and experience in your field and is familiar with your processes, software, and materials?"[2]

Remember, according to a 2010 Student Survey conducted by the National Association of Colleges and Employers, 51 percent of students have had internships by the time they graduate from college.[3] It would be disappointing to miss out on a job postcollege because the person you are up against had had an internship and you hadn't.

# NETWORKING

As an intern, your job is to meet all the people in the office and give them a reason to remember you. Potential contacts hear about job openings within their personal and professional networks, and you must be able to tap into those networks as an intern. Your ability to keep in touch with and nurture these contacts will be crucial to your long-term career goals. Do you know how I landed my first job out of college at Creative Artists Agency, the largest talent agency in the world? I called up a contact that I met at my FOX internship and asked him to put in a call for me. One week after moving to Los Angeles, I lined up an interview and landed the job. In chapters 8 and 9, I'll provide tons of networking tips to ensure you are able to properly leverage your new contacts.

# RESUME BUILDING

Employers judge candidates by this one piece of paper. If it doesn't list an internship and speak to the candidate's professionalism, experience, and capabilities, there is a strong chance it will get thrown away or deleted. I've termed these resumes "trash can resumes" and will continue to define what qualifies (and how to avoid) them in chapter 3. Employers spot an internship on a resume and they instantly see dedication, a strong work ethic, and a sense of focus from the student. Internships say to an employer, "I care about my future. I dedicated time to hone my skills and work on my craft in order to excel in my future."

My first out-of-state internship was in New York City at *Backstage*, a theatre trade newspaper. The day I phoned the company to ask about internship openings, the editor-in-chief, Sherry Eaker, answered the phone. Her first question was "Have you ever had an internship?" She was pleased when I answered, "Yes!" When a student's resume says "internship," it speaks to *experience*.

# REFERENCES

You should already know how to properly sell yourself—but do you have professionals willing to sell you? Are there executives who can speak intelligently and truthfully about your professional skills, attitude, and how you function in the workplace? Internships provide a place to gain these references and continuously prove yourself to a variety of professionals. Each task you perform has multiple purposes and will affect multiple people. Make sure each person you assist can speak to your capabilities. By doing this, you turn a *contact* into a *reference*. Jennifer Rupert, assistant director of Career Development at the New School in New York City explains, "People get to see you in action. They experience your work ethic and enthusiasm. In short, they get a chance to know you and become personally invested."[4]

These references will write you glowing letters of recommendation in the future. In other words, your relationships with internship coordinators and executives can drastically affect your future. Keep this in mind from day one of your internship.

# PURSUIT OR ELIMINATION

The last component of an internship is my favorite: pursuit or elimination. Students worry their internship experience might not be successful. But here's the thing, even less-than-stellar internships are beneficial. They establish what you *like* and what you *don't like*, what you want to pursue and what should be eliminated in terms of your future. Spend one semester interning at a company and determine if that's the right fit. Don't waste time doing this postcollege. Remember that experience—whether positive or negative—is still a valuable resume builder. No matter what the outcome, you will leave an internship more informed than when you walked in. You will gain knowledge of that industry, learn how the specific office is run, understand administrative tasks, and leave with contacts.

In 2005, I accepted an internship at NBC Universal in their on-air promotions department. The entertainment industry interested me, but I knew nothing about this specific part of the business. The internship provided a full education on the marketing and editing side of the television business. I spent my internship archiving old tapes, assisting in the edit bay, and helping the promotional spots go from idea to on the air. The entire process intrigued me but ultimately was not appealing enough to pursue after graduation. My internship allowed me to make great contacts in the marketing and on-air promotional space, learn a new side of the industry, and eventually decide that I didn't want to do this on a daily basis. I was grateful to learn that lesson as an intern for ten weeks instead of as an entry-level employee.

# TODAY'S INTERNSHIP SCENE

A few key factors have influenced the internship space the most over recent years. Internships are a frequent news topic with new terminology like perma-interns, alternative interns, intern contests, and even internship auctions being introduced. Every few years we also see a reality show or a television commercial emerge portraying interns in a variety of ways. Over the past year, I would even call internships trendy—as they are becoming "must haves" for today's college student. The economic downturn and changes in communication have led to more internship positions all over the world. More opportunities mean more students applying, and more students applying means employers are able to select from a higher caliber candidate pool.

## The Economic Effect

The surge of layoffs in early 2009 led to many more internship positions and a wider diversity of opportunities. Typically the most common internships are in the following fields: finance, engineering, marketing, sports, entertainment, education, nonprofit, media, journalism, publicity, sales, law, publishing, and medicine. Once the layoffs started, the number of available internship opportunities within these industries increased. The rise of entrepreneurship also created a new slew of internship opportunities for students at start-ups around the country.

The economic downturn also led to new criticisms that employers were firing employees and replacing them with interns. Employers have also been blamed for bringing students on for semester after semester and treating students as employees rather than as interns. A *perma-intern* is a student who stays at a company for multiple semesters and never leaves his or her internship. In chapter 6, I discuss legalities behind internships and talk more about this issue. It's important for employers to be aware of the internship guidelines and to understand that interns should not replace employees.

These days, most industries do offer some type of qualified internship experience. In fact, some companies like DKNY have gone so far as to auction off internships on eBay, something that stirred major controversy as this was considered "paying for an internship." The increase in internships not only in the United States but also abroad has also sparked students' interest. They see more opportunities, and more of them are willing to apply. For employers, more resumes coming in means they have a larger selection for their intern pools. The employers get to be more selective when they hire. Why not select a student who has previous experience?

With more students entering the job market with internships on their resumes, employers are able to hire more experienced candidates for entry-level jobs. This creates a strong demand for students to have internships before they graduate. Since universities want their students to grab top-notch positions, they must encourage their student body to intern. And if that means encouraging students as early as their freshman or sophomore years and mandating internship policies, they are going to do it. Several universities nationwide are considering new internship policies and shifting old ones. "Bradley University, for example, encourages first-year students to focus on internships and makes it possible for students to register for internship courses as soon as they have earned sophomore standing," explains Jane Linnenburger, executive director of Bradley University's Smith Career Center.[5] Another example is the Robert J. Trulaske, Sr., College of Business at the University of Missouri, the first of its kind to institute a mandatory internship program for undergraduate business majors.

The economy has not only affected the number of internships but also the types of internship candidates. The potential internship candidates who are not college students have been termed *alternative interns* and are hungry for work and experience. The typical internship candidate has historically been a college student, but now high school students, recent graduates, and adults have entered the space. High schools across America are creating internship programs for their students to gain college credits (similar to AP classes). Additionally adults who were laid off, stay-at-home moms, folks who went back to school or just want a career change are looking at internships. If you fall into the alternative intern category, follow the advice in the book just like a college student would. Many employers aren't used to taking on high school students, so a conversation should be had with the employer about their willingness to take on a high school intern. Another idea for high school students is to approach local business owners, as they may be more willing to hire them. Recent graduates and adults looking to change careers and utilize internships as a "foot in the door" should go after employers with informal human resource policies. A large company with a formal HR policy in place will not accept someone not enrolled in school. Below are a few tips for alternative interns to remember when using this book:

- Reach for the stars. There is always a way to get things done. Don't take no for an answer. If they say you cannot intern, ask if you can job shadow. If they say you cannot job shadow, ask to set up an informational interview.
- If you are in high school, ask your guidance counselor about programs the high school has established to help students find internship experience.
- Request informational interviews forever. I am out of school and I still reach out to people I admire and ask to sit down with them. You have a 50/50 chance they will say yes. The conversation might be life changing.
- Make sure you have a resume. If your resume hasn't been updated in a while, run it by your friend, counselor, or job coach. My mother's resume said she was married. Clearly it hadn't been updated in years.
- Don't let age play a part in your internship. Internship coordinators could be much older than you or much younger than you. No matter what their age, give them nothing but respect. If you are out of college and going into an internship, prepare to be very close in age to the internship coordinator. If you have a problem taking orders from someone younger than you, rethink interning.
- If you have heavy responsibility at home, consider a virtual internship position.
- If you cannot make the commitment to intern, consider asking someone for one of the lower-commitment approaches: job shadowing or informational interviewing.

# Changes in Communication

Another trend affecting the internship scene is the way we communicate. Our favorite ways to communicate have shifted dramatically over the past decade. We want our information and we know how to get it quickly. I'll never forget being in New York and hearing about an earthquake in Los Angeles (where I currently live). Do you know how I found out? Twitter. When I checked CNN and other news sites, nothing was up. Twitter provided me with an instant real-time newsfeed. From Twitter updates to Facebook status and Foursquare check-ins, the way we communicate now is extremely different from how we've communicated in the past. The internship space does a pretty decent job of adapting to this technology friendly environment. Indeed, communication has changed both the tasks at internships and how students find opportunities.

An example of this is the *Twitern*, a phrase Pizza Hut coined for their Twitter-friendly internship position. Yes, they hire an intern to monitor the brand's public persona on Twitter. Employers need students on board who have already integrated social media into their daily lifestyle and who can do the same thing for the company's brand. Students use Facebook, MySpace, Twitter, LinkedIn, and Foursquare every day, so they understand how to make a brand's social media profile come alive.

Communication also affects the way students find internships. Whereas before, a clear barrier existed between student and recruiter, companies and brands now favor personalized online connections. The relationship between consumer and brand is more intimate than in the past. Brands spend hundreds of thousands of dollars each year hiring people to log on to the Internet and start a conversation. Students should have an online relationship with brands and employers that interest them. Top recruiters like Starbucks, AT&T, and Limited brands all have this functionality. They want to engage students through unique online platforms. Social media has definitely become one of the most talked about topics in the business. I'll speak more on how to connect with target employers through social media in chapter 4.

The trends mentioned above propose challenges to you, the student. Employers review resumes and look for more internship experience, more extracurricular activities, and overall a more qualified candidate. Can you be this candidate? Do you have what it takes?

# FINDING TIME FOR AN INTERNSHIP

Throughout my speaking tours, students always ask me how they can fit an internship into their busy schedules. They already attend classes, work part-time, and want to have fun. I'm here to tell you that it *is* all possible. Developing strong time management skills will help you learn how to fit an internship into your life. It's all a matter of focus and preparation. I instruct you to divide and conquer. First, let's figure out how you currently spend your time. When I was a student, I didn't fully understand how I spent my time, so I tracked all of my activities (even eating and sleeping) throughout the period of one week. During my junior year of college, I interned at Transcontinental Media, had four school classes per week, and waited tables at the Improv Comedy Club in Orlando. My schedule looked something like the schedule at the top of the opposite page.

And below that is an example of my schedule from the summer after my sophomore year of college when I interned in Los Angeles at two companies (BWR Public Relations and Warren Cowan & Associates). I also worked part-time at Islands Fine Burgers.

If you have trouble prioritizing, time management expert Elizabeth Saunders says, "If you feel overwhelmed, list out everything on your plate, from friends to meetings. Then put these in order of importance based on two criteria:

- Does it bring you toward your professional and personal goals?
- Does it make you happy and bring you energy?

## SAMPLE SCHEDULE

| Monday | Tuesday | Wednesday | Thursday | Friday | Saturday | Sunday |
|--------|---------|-----------|----------|--------|----------|--------|
| Communication Classes 7:45 a.m.– Noon | Internship @ Transcontinental Media 9:00 a.m.– 2:00 p.m. | Communication Classes 7:45 a.m.– Noon | Internship @ Transcontinental Media 9:00 a.m.– 2:00 p.m. | Communication Classes 7:45 a.m.– Noon | Shopping or brunch with friends | Sleep in! & Study Day— all day! |
| Internship @ Transcontinental Media 1:30 p.m.– 5:30 p.m. | FREE TIME 2:00 p.m.– 6:00 p.m. | Internship @ Transcontinental Media 1:30 p.m.– 5:30 p.m. | FREE TIME 2:00 p.m.– 6:00 p.m. | FREE TIME 12:00 p.m.– 6:30 p.m. | Catch up on random assignments | Study, study, study for the week. |
| Work @ Improv Comedy Club 6:30 p.m.– 11:30 p.m. | Class 6:00 p.m.– 9:45 p.m. | Work @ Improv Comedy Club 6:30 p.m.– 11:30 p.m. | Class 6:00 p.m.– 9:45 p.m. | Work @ Improv Comedy Club 6:30 p.m.– 11:30 p.m. | Go to bookstore café to study and hang out | Work @ Improv Comedy Club 6:30 p.m.– 11:30 p.m. |
| | FREE TIME & STUDY TIME 10:00 p.m.– Midnight | | Go out with friends after class OR study time | | Go out with friends around 10:00 p.m. usually | |

## SAMPLE SCHEDULE

| Monday | Tuesday | Wednesday | Thursday | Friday | Saturday | Sunday |
|--------|---------|-----------|----------|--------|----------|--------|
| Internship at BWR Public Relations 9:00 a.m.– 5:00 p.m. | FREE TIME | Internship at BWR Public Relations 9:00 a.m.– 5:00 p.m. | Internship @ Warren Cowan & Associates 9:00 a.m.– 5:00 p.m. | Internship @ Warren Cowan & Associates 9:00 a.m.– 5:00 p.m. | FREE TIME for sightseeing in Los Angeles | Work @ Islands Fine Burgers 10:00 a.m.– 3:00 p.m. |
| Work @ Islands Fine Burgers 6:00 p.m.– 11:00 p.m. | FREE TIME | Work @ Islands Fine Burgers 6:00 p.m.– 11:00 p.m. | FREE TIME | Work @ Islands Fine Burgers 6:00 p.m.– 11:00 p.m. | Work @ Islands Fine Burgers 4:00 p.m.– 11:00 p.m. | FREE TIME and usually movie night! |

## BLANK SCHEDULE

| Monday | Tuesday | Wednesday | Thursday | Friday | Saturday | Sunday |
|--------|---------|-----------|----------|--------|----------|--------|
|        |         |           |          |        |          |        |
|        |         |           |          |        |          |        |
|        |         |           |          |        |          |        |

## PRIORITY LIST

1.
2.
3.
4.
5.
6.
7.
8.
9.
10.

If at all possible, eliminate or at least minimize the time you spend on anything that falls at the bottom of the list."[6] I've inserted a blank calendar on the opposite page for you to fill out followed by a priority list. Remember, first fill out the calendar and then prioritize and take a close look at where your time is being spent.

Once you've listed and estimated the time requirements of your commitments and eliminated nonessential items, the next step is to create a close-to-perfect class schedule. I've attended two large universities (Florida State University and University of Central Florida), so I know this isn't always possible or realistic. Attempt to stack your classes on certain days of the week. Try putting all of your classes on Monday, Wednesday, Friday or Tuesdays and Thursdays. This way you can intern for full business days in between. Another option is to schedule all of your classes early in the morning so that you are able to intern in the afternoons. Remember, the business day is usually 8 or 9 a.m. until 5 or 6 p.m. Most internships require at least fifteen hours per week, so working five-hour shifts for three days per week could be an option. You could also intern every day of the week for three hours each day. When I was in school, I would schedule evening classes twice per week so that I could intern for two full days in the office. To make sure that school remains a priority, do not start your internship until your class schedule is confirmed. Even if your internship coordinator asks you to start your internship early, I encourage you to ask if you can wait until the second week of classes. This will show the employer that personal organization is a priority.

Additional options for students feeling constantly strapped for time are online classes and virtual internships. If flexibility is a priority, I suggest you check out these opportunities on your campus. With virtual internships, you can work from home or school and communicate with the company online, over the phone, or by using Skype. Virtual interns perform a variety of tasks; the only real difference is the internship takes place off-site. Virtual interns can be responsible for marketing plans, press strategy, website management, administrative work, social media, and a variety of other tasks. This is an interesting option for students who need to be at home during the day, live far away from metropolitan areas, or want a more flexible internship schedule. The number of virtual internship listings on my website has tripled over the past year.

Part-time jobs may be a necessary component for your internship process. Many students participating in unpaid internships must find part-time work to support their summers. Also, many students (including myself) manage an internship, part-time job, and schoolwork during the school year. If you decide to take the plunge and get a great internship *and* part-time job, you must run a tight ship and conduct yourself in a professional manner. Find a job that works for your schedule, not against it. You'll want to find a job that brings in a decent paycheck, forces you to meet new people, and is convenient. Don't take a job because it's the first one you see or because all of your friends work there. You don't want your job to be a stress factor in your life. Do whatever it takes to find the right opportunity for you and your schedule.

When I was a student, I don't think I understood the value of my time or that I had the ability to say no to friends and events. I found myself always saying *yes* and never having any time to myself. Often we are sucked into other people's worlds, and before we know it, our entire day is spent catering to someone else's schedule.

Make this year about concentrating on *your* life and building your own schedule. Decide how you want to spend your time, what your priorities are, and put your schedule together—one commitment at a time. Gabrielle Bernstein, author of *Spirit Junkie*, also supports this theory and says, "Scale back. The key to managing a few things at once is to keep it to *a few*. Learning how to say no is crucial. Keep it simple and you'll find that you'll have more energy and more time to do great work."[7]

## 👑 INTERN QUEEN CHAPTER ESSENTIALS

- Review and make sure you fully understand the five components behind any internship: hands-on education, networking, resume building, gaining references, and pursuit or elimination.

- Have a clear understanding of how the economy and communication have affected the number of internships, how people get them, and what you need to do to be competitive.
- Track and write down how you spend your time for one week. Decide which activities are worth your time and which aren't. Make a new schedule and determine how many hours per week you should be spending on each activity. Don't forget to sleep!
- Create your close-to-perfect class schedule. Block out a few hours one night to mess around with your class schedule and the days you take classes. Look at all of the options such as days of the week, evening classes, or morning classes.
- Check out online classes at your college or university if you think this could be a viable option for you.
- Decide if you will get a part-time job and start looking for some possibilities.
- Research virtual internships and consider them an option if you have a tough schedule, need to work from home, or feel your local opportunities are limited.

After fully disclosing the advantages of taking internships, showing you trends within the internship space, and proving that you can make time for internships, let's continue. Feel free to flip back and review these five components whenever you get an internship offer. The rest of the book takes you through the internship application process and the actual internship opportunity. My goal is to get you prepared and make you a knowledgeable internship candidate who understands the entire process from day one until the last day. With my help, you will become the ideal intern candidate.

As the Intern Queen, I've had my fair share of internship experiences. I hope I've relayed the momentous role they've played in my life. Everything I absorbed from my internships helped build the foundation for my professional career. And now I'd like to officially pass the torch down to you, the intern candidate. It's your turn to experience the power that these internships provide. Are you ready for your click moment?

# Find and Land
# Your Dream
# Internship

*At the University of Central Florida,* I lived with three girls in your typical four-by-four college apartment. We got along great, enjoying many nights at the Library (the tongue-in-cheek name of the local pub), cooking family-style dinners, and watching our favorite television shows. My roommates went to school and worked part-time jobs at TGI Fridays. My lifestyle was different. I juggled twelve credit hours at school, an internship, a part-time job at the Orlando Improv, and wrote articles for *Us Weekly*, *Seventeen*, and *Nickelodeon* magazine.

One evening I came home from my job and plopped down on the couch, exhausted from running around all day. My roommates sat on the opposite side of the couch, staring at me. I laughed, "What? Do I look dead?" I asked. "I certainly feel it."

"Lauren, you're so busy all of the time and you've had all of these internships. We haven't had any internships. How did you get so many?" one of the girls blurted out, as if it were a secret, or something they'd discussed before I came inside.

They looked up at me like they were expecting an enlightening response of some sort.

"Ummmm. . . ." I paused, not knowing how to respond to the question. "Honestly, I just picked where I wanted to work and found a way to work or intern there. . . ." I trailed off, thinking about my experiences, which, at that point, totaled ten internships.

My roommate's response was, "Well, no one ever told us *how* to intern somewhere. . . ." They looked back at me with blank stares.

To this day, that conversation sticks with me. I wanted to shake my roommates and say, "You can do this too. You can do anything you want to do." But I didn't. And, unfortunately, neither did anyone else. Even though we attended the third largest university in the country, with some of the best student resources, the career center couldn't possibly reach every student and find each one the perfect internship. And so my roommates never ended up getting internships, leaving them with limited opportunities after college. They could have interned and experienced the same life-changing experiences that I had, but they didn't seek out any positions. They had no sense of urgency. Perhaps this is characteristic of our generation. But let's break the stereotype—let's become a generation known for *making* things happen.

I feel guilty for not encouraging my roommates to intern and not being an additional source of motivation to help them achieve their goals. Let me be this person for *you*. The person who says, "You *can* get the internship of your dreams, and this is how." Like every journey, the most difficult part is the first step—just getting off the couch. Don't just talk about getting an internship. You must take action and follow the necessary steps to find, land, and make the most of an opportunity.

In this chapter, I'll teach you how to strategically organize your applications so that you can track and monitor all of the internships for which you apply. This entire process revolves around the Intern Queen Dream List, a document I created and utilized to stay on top of internship applications, target specific employers, meet deadlines, and, ultimately, land a position. In the following sections, I break down each part of the Intern Queen Dream List: company, company website, contact information, required materials, deadline, date sent, and follow-up. You need to understand exactly what information to write on this list and where to find it.

## INTERN QUEEN DREAM LIST

| Company Name | Website | Contact | Materials Required | Deadline | Date Sent | Follow-Up Date |
|---|---|---|---|---|---|---|
| | | | | | | |
| | | | | | | |
| | | | | | | |
| | | | | | | |
| | | | | | | |
| | | | | | | |
| | | | | | | |
| | | | | | | |
| | | | | | | |
| | | | | | | |

## SAMPLE INTERN QUEEN DREAM LIST

| Company Name | Website | Contact (Names Changed) | Materials Required | Deadline | Date Sent | Follow-Up Date |
|---|---|---|---|---|---|---|
| *Tallahassee* magazine | www.tallahasseemagazine.com | Lauren Gold | R, CL | Mar. 15 | Mar. 1 | Mar. 17 |
| Moore Public Relations | www.moore-pr.com | Shannon Howard | R, CL | Feb. 1 | Jan. 20 | Feb. 3 |
| *Tallahassee Democrat* | www.tallahassee.com | Lauren Clemmons | R | Mar. 15 | Mar. 1 | Mar. 17 |
| *Backstage* newspaper | www.backstage.com | Michael Kenny | R | Rolling | Mar. 1 | Mar. 17 |
| *Paper* magazine | www.papermag.com | Abby Art | R, CL, writing samples | Mar. 15 | Mar. 1 | Mar. 17 |
| *Seventeen* magazine | www.seventeen.com | Rori Wolfe | R | Feb. 1 | Jan. 20 | Feb. 3 |
| BWR Public Relations | www.bwr-pr.com | Ashley Silberman | R, CL | Mar. 15 | Mar. 1 | Mar. 17 |
| The *Village Voice* | www.villagevoice.com | Samantha Nifakos | R, CL, letters of recommendation | Mar. 1 | Jan. 20 | Mar. 3 |
| *Cosmopolitan* magazine | www.cosmopolitan.com | Jonathan David | R, CL, writing samples | Nov. 15 | Nov. 1 | Nov. 20 |

I've included two Intern Queen Dream Lists in this book (see previous two pages). One is blank and for you to fill out as you go through this chapter. The other is a sample of what my dream list looked like as I went after my second internship, during my freshman year of college. I looked for opportunities both locally in Tallahassee and in New York City for the summer. Think of the Intern Queen Dream List document as your roadmap for the entire application process. I promise, it will take you from where you are to where you want to be. The list is referenced throughout the book, and I encourage you to fill it out in its entirety. It will help you define exactly where you want to intern, research those employers, and organize all of the requirements for their applications.

# DREAM LIST SECTION #1:
## The Company

To help fill out your dream list ask yourself, "What is my dream job?" If your major, financial situation, and location were not an issue, where do you visualize yourself working and being happy in the future? Take this moment to be creative and let your mind go. Don't confine yourself to any industry. Remember, this isn't about what your parents, teachers, or friends want for you. It's all about what you want for yourself.

When I told my mom and my dad—who have had lifelong careers as a dentist and a high school teacher, respectively—that I wanted to be the Intern Queen, they thought I was crazy. And they weren't the only ones. My friends and coworkers laughed at me when I told them I was creating a site to help college students land internships. Unfortunately family and friends will not always support you. Go with your gut instinct. What are *you* passionate about? This is your life.

### Don't Be Held Hostage by Your Major

Students often feel restricted by their majors. Recently I had a student who was a business management major ask me if she could apply for a film internship. Of course! Go after what you want, no matter what your major might be. In many cases, schools force students to declare majors before they are confident in what they want to do. When creating your dream list, think big, and consider any potential career choice that interests you. In chapter 3, I discuss cover letters, and that is when I'll focus on how to properly address applying for a position outside of your major.

When I spoke at Northwood University in Midlands, Michigan, a student named Stacey cautiously raised her hand during my Q&A session. I knew she was self-conscious. "The truth is, I'm a senior and about to graduate and I don't know what I want to do. I just don't know. What should I do?"

"Oh, Stacey," I responded immediately, "Repeat after me, *it is okay*. I guarantee that at least ten other students in this room feel the same way."

I asked the students in the room who were unsure of what they wanted to do to raise their hands. As expected, more than ten hands shot up. I told Stacey that when I was a freshman, I felt clueless about what I wanted to do with my life.

To help Stacey get a better sense of direction for her own plans postgraduation, I shared the method I used when beginning my internship search. As a freshman at Florida State University, I printed out a list of the majors that the school had to offer and circled what I was drawn to. I circled advertising, marketing, public relations, public affairs, creative writing, film, and meteorology. I never understood where meteorology came from—oh well. But the others all had something to do with the communications field— clue! I was one step closer to figuring out a potential career choice. I knew my first internship should incorporate a field from my list.

Below I've listed the ten most popular majors at colleges and universities according to the *Princeton Review*. Circle the majors that appeal to you. Or write in other fields of interest alongside my list.

- Business administration and management or commerce
- Psychology
- Nursing
- Biology or biological sciences
- Education
- English language and literature

- Economics
- Communications studies or speech rhetoric
- Political science and government
- Computer and information sciences[1]

Another way to find out which industry best suits you is to speak with friends and family. Their thoughts and ideas might surprise you. People always asked what I wanted to be when I grew up. My grandma would normally answer for me in her heavy Brooklyn accent, "Lauren is going to be a writer." I laughed it off. My grandma took my writing awards as a child to mean that I would eventually blossom into a professional writer. My mother always told me I should be a speaker. As I write this book and think about the number of speeches I've given across the country, I can't help but think that my mother and grandma knew something I didn't. Although family and friends might not always support your ideas and career path, they often recognize your strengths and are worth speaking to about your future.

## Know Your Experience Level

Before you can determine the specific employers to pursue, determine your experience level so you understand the type of positions for which you should apply. Generally, competitive internship programs want to see experience on your resume. Look at the different types of internship experience levels below: newbie intern, in-between intern, and almost an Intern Queen. See which best describes your current experience level.

### NEWBIE INTERN
This is your first internship. You are probably an underclassman or perhaps you're a senior, just starting to focus on your future. You have no relevant experience; your resume includes some part-time jobs and a few extracurricular activities. Your dream list will consist of local companies. If you want to go out of state, focus on smaller boutique employers, which usually specialize in one specific industry and have only a handful of executives.

You need to get that first internship under your belt to help you land bigger names for the following semester.

## IN-BETWEEN INTERN

You've had a local internship so your resume isn't blank under "previous experience." You might be ready to go after that out-of-state opportunity now that you have some relevant experience. Your dream list will include a combination of local and national opportunities. Remember, the highly competitive internships look for relevant experience on your resume. If your first internship was in a similar field, you will have a better chance of landing a big brand-name internship.

## ALMOST AN INTERN QUEEN

You have a few internships under your belt, either out of state or with big brand names. You keep aiming higher and higher. Be proud of yourself. As far as employers go, think as large as you want. Go after the most competitive internships in the marketplace and fill up *that* dream list with great employers! Good luck!

## Large Employer vs. Small Employer

Make sure you don't apply for only big-name employers. A common myth is that large employers always provide a better experience than smaller companies. The quality of the internship depends on the specific company and how much effort it puts into its internship program. It also depends on how much effort you, the student, put into your internship. Make sure that you apply to a variety of employers, both large and small. Students tend to apply for the company names that they recognize. For example, *Seventeen* magazine and Interscope Records are the two most popular internships on my site, generating thousands of applicants. Students limit themselves when they only apply for big name opportunities. When looking over internship listings on my site, at school, or online, read as many listings as possible. Focus on the details of the internship posting, not just the name listed at the top. Company names might be foreign to you, so take a moment to google the company; you might be surprised by what you find.

## Finding the Specific Employers

What happens when you don't know what companies you want to put on your dream list? Below are a few resources to check to find internship opportunities.

### RESOURCE #1: VISIT YOUR CAREER CENTER

Before you look for internship opportunities anywhere else, go into your school's career center. Look on the school website or ask a professor where the career center is located on your campus. Most colleges and universities either have a centralized career center that covers all majors or a decentralized career center that exists within each major or department. The career center professionals build relationships with local, national, and international employers so that those employers hire their students for jobs and internships. Colleges want to brag about their graduates' placement statistics via the on-campus career center. They want to help you find the right opportunities.

Beth Shapiro Settje, internship resources manager at the Department of Career Services at the University of Connecticut says, "Whether the student has an idea of a specific job, company, or industry, chances are that someone working at the college's career center has a relevant connection." She goes on to provide students with some tips for using the career center: "Get to know the career services staff to stay connected. Many times employers contact us directly looking for candidates. Why not be at the top of the list when we are sharing information and suggesting candidates? Ideally students will start developing a relationship with the career services staff in their first or second year of school."[2] She encourages students to attend the networking and career-related events that the career center puts on to help students best leverage their skills and land great opportunities.

Go in with a copy of your Intern Queen Dream List and ask them to help you identify employers to write on your list.

## RESOURCE #2: ONLINE

I started my site, www.internqueen.com, to create a free internship listing site that is large in reach but still feels niche and personalized. Currently I work with thousands of employers in communications, marketing, fashion, public relations, entertainment, journalism, tech, and start-ups.

I also recommend checking out larger job boards that aggregate positions from a variety of different places; these include www.indeed.com, www.simplyhired.com, and www.juju.com. The internship listings on my site, as well as from other internship sites, appear on these large search engines, so they are a great place to start your search.

In chapter 4, I will discuss using social media (Facebook, Twitter, LinkedIn) to locate available internship opportunities.

## RESOURCE #3: MY "PICK IT AND LAND IT" THEORY

My favorite method of internship hunting, "pick it and land it," contradicts the advice of most career coaches and job guides. In such a crowded marketplace, you must focus on what you *want* and not what is *available*. Several employers have their own Applicant Tracking Systems (ATS) and don't put their internship postings on websites other than their own. Other employers use word of mouth to publicize opportunities and don't have online listings anywhere.

When I was in college, there weren't many strong internship resources. I went to my good friend www.google.com. In my situation, it was a matter of typing in "public relations companies in Tallahassee, Florida." Two of the companies I interned for still come up when I do that search, the Zimmerman Agency and Moore Public Relations. Don't copy down everything you find on Google without first visiting the company website. Research the company before you put it on your dream List. A dream list filled with spam is no help to anyone. Exceptional internship candidates know exactly what they are applying for before the application goes out.

# DREAM LIST SECTION #2:
# Company Website

I included "Website" on the Intern Queen Dream List so you actually visit the company website before sending out your materials. This initiates the research portion of your internship search. Career books suggest doing the research before going into an interview. In my opinion, it's imperative to do the research before submitting applications. What if the internship responsibilities aren't what you assumed they'd be? What if they offer you the internship and you realize you don't even want to intern there? Do the research before submitting your applications; it doesn't take long and will save you time.

## Starting Your Company Research on the Website

- Go to the company website and click About Us. Read the company history and the executives' biographies.
- Look for the company mission statement (most companies have one), which clearly explains the overall goal of the employer. Pay close attention to the language and wording the company uses to describe itself. In chapters 3 and 5, I'll explain how to incorporate parts of the mission statement into your cover letter and interview.
- Check out the company's clients to familiarize yourself with the types of businesses with which it works. Most websites have a category titled Clients.
- The final step of the research process is going to Google, clicking News, and typing in the company name to see what comes up. For example, if this were 2008, when the financial crisis hit, you wouldn't want to apply for internships at Lehman Brothers or AIG. Use Google alerts (www.google.com/alerts) to tell you about a company and its clients. Has the company lost a client recently? You might read that a talent agency just fired or lost a client, so you wouldn't want to

bring up that client's name at your interview. Find these things out ahead of time.

If you encounter an *on-the-spot interview*, an instance where an employer, to whom you've submitted an application, calls you without notice, you'll want to be prepared. These types of interviews happen when an employer wants to see that you know what you are applying for. Have you done the research ahead of time? Keep in mind that employers may ask, "Have you gone to our website?" If you say no, you're not only unprepared, but you've also lessened your chances of landing the internship.

To prevent being caught off guard, make sure you read the actual internship listing and visit the company website before you actually apply. Blind applications shouldn't exist. Make notes on your dream list to help you remember each company and what it does. I also suggest carrying your dream list around with you in your backpack or bag so that if an employer calls and you are walking around campus or at a friend's house, you can pull it out, refresh your memory, and come across as well prepared.

# DREAM LIST SECTION #3:
## Contact Info

Once you have ten companies on your Intern Queen Dream List, go to each company's website to find the appropriate contact information. On the majority of websites, you can locate internship information under the Careers, Jobs, Internships, About Us, or Our People section. However, that's not the case on all websites. If you cannot find any sort of career information on the employer website, go back to Google. I'll stick with the Zimmerman Agency example. If I go to their website, www.zimmerman.com, there is no contact information for internships (still). When I go back to Google and type "internships at the Zimmerman Agency," I find a few job boards where the agency has listed its internship information and a recently updated blog post from a local Tallahassee website that includes the specific internship listing with the internship coordinator's contact information.

Whenever you find an actual contact name and email address on a website that has been updated within the past six months, that's always a good sign. There are three things you want to include under the Contact section on the Intern Queen Dream List: the internship coordinator's name, email address, and direct phone number. If this information isn't available, write in the company general phone number, which is always found on the company website.

## To Cold-Call or Not to Cold-Call

In general, employers do not suggest cold-calling. However, I'm an advocate of breaking the rules. I suggest cold-calling under the following circumstances:

- You cannot find any information on the internship opportunities at the company.
- You cannot find the name or email of an internship coordinator at the company.
- You emailed a generic company email address and have not heard a response from anyone at the company.

Here are a few pointers to remember when cold-calling employers:

- Before you call, have a notepad and pen in front of you to take notes. You don't want to have to call back because you failed to write down the information.
- Speak clearly, at the appropriate volume, and slowly. Don't let your nerves affect your pace.
- Normally, if you are calling a general number for an employer, you are dialing the main receptionist. These people oftentimes don't have a department list. When you call, ask to speak with the internship coordinator. The receptionist will either connect you to that person or lead you to a place on the website where you can apply. Make sure you go to the website before making this call. If the receptionist points

you to a place that doesn't exist on the site, let her know. Tell her you are happy to hold while she asks someone else how you might apply for an internship with the company or speak with the internship coordinator. Don't let yourself get frustrated with the receptionist. It isn't worth your time, and you never know who they might know.

- Be prepared for internship coordinators to tell you the positions are filled for that year. If they say this, I recommend asking when the best time would be to apply for the following semester or the following year's opportunities. You can plan ahead for the future and make sure you don't miss future deadlines. Remember, you have a list of at least nine other companies for which you are applying. If you cannot get through to one of them, it's not the end of the world.

- Be polite but assertive. You walk a fine line between being persistent and being annoying. You can't fall on the annoying side! Remember, you never know with whom you are speaking. Make sure you listen carefully to whomever you are speaking with. Try not to step on their words. Avoid telling personal stories unless you are asked, sounding entitled to the position, sounding agitated with the person on the phone, or putting the internship coordinator on the spot by pitching yourself too hard. Remember, your materials are going to speak for you. Stay professional.

- The internship coordinator's voicemail might come up when you call. Try to write down the internship coordinator's name so that if you don't receive a return call, you can call the coordinator back to follow up in one week. Also, use this opportunity to find out the contact person's full name. You might only know this person as "internship coordinator" before hearing the voicemail. Leave a pleasant-sounding message like the following:

Hello, this is Lauren Berger. My number is 555-555-5555. I was calling to get more information about applying to your summer internship program. I'm a junior at the University of Central Florida.

Thanks so much. Again, my number is 555-555-5555.

- Make a note in your calendar of the day you called and place a follow-up call one full week after. I suggest that you avoid making follow-up calls on Monday mornings or Friday afternoons. Employers are playing catch-up from the weekend on Monday mornings and have usually dialed out by Friday afternoon.
- When you call back, you can say, "Hello. I'm following up on the message I left you a few days ago regarding internship opportunities at your company. I'd love to apply."
- On the notepad, write down the following example conversation to help guide you:

**Receptionist:** Hello, (company name)
**You:** Hello. I'd like to speak with the internship coordinator, please.
**Receptionist:** Please hold.
**Internship Coordinator:** Hello.
**You:** Hi, my name is Lauren Berger and I attend University of Central Florida. I wanted to find out how to apply for a summer internship at your company.
**Internship Coordinator:** Sure. Just send your resume over to me via email. My email is internshipcoordinator@gmail.com.
**You:** Great. Thank you so much.

# DREAM LIST SECTION #4:
# Materials Required

Use this section to write in the application materials required for each internship position. The majority of employers will just ask for a resume. Always send your resume along with a cover letter, even if the employer doesn't ask for it. It doesn't hurt to provide the employer with more information on your specific situation, availability, and strengths. Also check to see if the employer specifies a format for your materials. The most popular formats are PDF and Word docs. If one format is specified, you must follow the guidelines. If you do not, the employer might delete your materials as you've already shown that you cannot follow the rules. Make sure that whatever you are sending is compatible with both Macs and PCs. If a specific format is not specified, I suggest attaching both a PDF and Word doc for the convenience of the employer. Employers often require letters of recommendation, transcripts, writing samples, or portfolios (hard copy or online). I refer to these as "the extras" and will discuss them in more depth in chapter 3.

# DREAM LIST SECTION #5: Deadline

When you apply for colleges, some have specific deadlines and others have *rolling admissions*, meaning they accept applicants at different points throughout the year. Internships are the same way. While many employers will accept applicants on a rolling basis, the most popular internship deadlines are November 1 for the spring and March 15 for summer. But be aware, long-lead summer internship deadlines are November 1!

If you don't see a strict deadline date on the company website or on the internship listing, here are some calendar rules to follow.

## Summer Internship Deadlines

The normal summer internship runs from mid-June until the second week of August. Keep in mind, the dates depend on school calendars and applicant availability. On the West Coast, schools tend to get out later in the year so internships for those students start later. Summer internships end between the first week of August and the last week of August, depending on when you started. Apply for summer internships as early in the year as possible. March 15 is always a good deadline to have in your mind.

Now, there are internships that have early summer deadlines of November 1. The *Washington Post* and the *New York Times* are two competitive internships that boast early deadlines. Get a head start on your summer internship search and start looking up deadlines as soon as you begin school in the fall. Make sure you don't miss out because you didn't prepare early enough!

# Fall Internship Deadlines

Fall internships start after Labor Day and last until right after Thanksgiving break. Normally the internship ends the second week of December, right before exams. If employers list no deadline, submit applications for these in June and July. They select their interns by the beginning of September, at the latest.

## Winter Internship Deadlines

Students who go after *winternships* (as I like to call them), or winter internships, are normally on the quarter system or have a longer-than-usual winter break. Harvard, for example, has an intersession and gives students the entire month of January off. A winternship would be ideal for a Harvard student. Winternships range from after Thanksgiving until after New Year's Day. They cut off before Christmas, since many companies are closed for the majority of the holidays. Employers select winter interns, or *winterns*, around the same time as spring interns. Apply for these positions after Labor Day and explain when you will be available to an employer. The latest date for submitting winter internship applications should be right before Thanksgiving. Andrea, one of my Intern Queen Campus Ambassadors from Ohio University, did a *winternship* at *Marie Claire* magazine in December. She interned from right after Thanksgiving until right before Christmas for five days per week, ten hours per day, and was able to receive school credit.

## Spring Internship Deadlines

Spring internships start between the first week of January and the middle of February, depending on the student's academic schedule. They typically run through the end of the student's spring term in April or May. Normally an internship wraps up a week before the student has their final exams. Submit applications for spring by mid-October if no deadline is listed. Most employers will try to select their spring internship candidates before Thanksgiving. Employers running late will select spring candidates all the way up until February 15.

# DREAM LIST SECTION #6:
## Date Sent

Block out time to send out all of your applications over the period of one week. Realistically you probably need two days where you can block out four hours each day. I'm a huge fan of blocking out big chunks of time to complete projects. This helps you easily organize and keep track of your applications. Since you must customize all of your materials for each position, I would allow approximately forty-five minutes per application (assuming you already have your resume done). This gives you time to research the company and write a new version of your cover letter. We will talk more specifically about customized cover letters in the next chapter.

# DREAM LIST SECTION #7:
## Follow Up

You have to follow up. Internship coordinators are not always stand-alone, meaning they are often midlevel or entry-level executives tasked with finding interns. They juggle multiple projects and don't always have interns at the top of their priority list. Follow-up emails are helpful reminders for busy internship coordinators. Unfortunately, if you mail or email your resume through a large applicant tracking system on a company website or job board, you are normally unable to follow up as there is no one to follow up with. However, if you send your materials to an actual person (under the Contact section of your Intern Queen Dream List) then you should absolutely follow up by email exactly two weeks after you sent your materials, as long as it's after the application deadline. Look at your Date Sent category and mark the date that you will need to follow up with the employer. Avoid sending follow-up emails on Mondays and Fridays as Mondays tend to be busy days in the office and Fridays tend to be days when nothing gets done. After writing the follow-up date on your dream list, send the email and highlight the row. Stay organized during this process so you do not accidentally double email employers. Follow-up notes should be short and sweet reminders to the employer that you are still interested and awaiting their response. Do not fill these notes with loaded questions such as "When will I hear from you?" or "When will you make a decision?" The note should serve as a friendly reminder, nothing that makes the employer feel pressured to make a quick decision. Follow-up should be done by email instead of phone as you don't want to put the employer on the spot and interrupt the flow of the work day. The employer can answer an email when its convenient.

My younger brother, Jonathan, graduated from the University of Central Florida and works for an investment bank—thanks to great internship experience and networking. Poor Jonathan dealt with his sister being the Intern Queen throughout his four years of college. I spoke with Jonathan his sophomore year of college and told him it was time to jump on the internship bandwagon with his sister. He could be the Intern King! I asked if he'd applied to any internships. His vague response was, "Yeah, I applied for a few but never heard back."

"Um, okay, so did you email to follow up?" I asked in my most annoying sister voice.

"No, LB. I didn't."

Jonathan knew he was in for a lecture and pulled up the email applications he'd sent to a handful of financial firms.

"This is great, Jonathan, but if you don't follow up you are wasting your time. The employer isn't thinking about the interns all day. You need to follow up and bring this back to their attention."

Jonathan followed my advice and sent a short follow-up email to all of the employers. His email to Morgan Stanley Smith Barney read:

Bob,

I attend the University of Central Florida and applied for the spring internship with your company on November 10. I wanted to follow up with you and see if you required any additional materials. I've attached my resume and cover letter again. I look forward to speaking with you further.

Best,
Jonathan Berger

Jonathan received an email from Bob the following day requesting an interview. He landed the internship. If he hadn't followed up, would he have landed the internship? We'll never know.

You can send one follow-up email, and if you still get no response, move on to the other internships on your list. That's why you research and apply to multiple companies. If you get rejected, you can move right along to the next opportunity.

Now that we've finished going through the sections of the Intern Queen Dream List, I want to discuss using a calendar system so that you can track all of your important dates.

# CREATE YOUR CALENDAR SYSTEM

We now have several important dates to remember: when you actually send out applications, company deadlines, and follow-up days. The best way to track these dates is setting up a calendar. Your email server should have a calendar linked to it, and your cell phone should have calendar functionality as well. Start treating yourself like the professional you want to become. As an executive, you will need a daily calendar to stay organized and on top of commitments. If you are a visual person, maybe you'll use a planner so that you can write everything down. I personally use a Google Calendar (it's free!) and link it with my Blackberry. Find a way to stay organized and keep it updated. I use the same calendar for personal and professional commitments. I can't book a speaking engagement on the same day as a friend's wedding or an interview at the same time as a dinner.

In your calendar, mark the important dates you'll need to remember.

- Write down all of the appointments you've made with the career center staff over the next few months.
- Note the deadlines listed for each company on your Intern Queen Dream List.
- Identify *long-lead internships* (internships that have deadlines over four months ahead of time) and block out time to get your materials

together and send your applications. Allow six hours total to work on your resume and cover letter and another three hours for the application send-out process. Decide when you will do this and write the dates and times down in your calendar.

- Make yourself a mock deadline of fifteen days before the actual deadline. If the internship deadline is November 1, your deadline would be October 15. This will ensure that you aren't stressed-out at the last minute.
- Write down the date you plan to follow up with an employer. Remember, this should be two full weeks after you send an initial application to the employer.
- Add in any personal commitments or events you have coming up. I suggest putting professional items and personal items in the same place so you can keep your life in order. We all have lots on our plate!

## 👑 INTERN QUEEN CHAPTER ESSENTIALS

- Identify which experience-level category you fall under (newbie, in between, almost an Intern Queen) to help you decide which types and sizes of internships to apply for.
- Think about your dream job. Speak to family and friends and get their opinions on what career choice they think you should pursue. You don't need to take their advice, but do consider it.
- Print out a list of college majors if you are undecided on your career choice. Circle what interests you.
- Make a copy of the blank Intern Queen Dream List on page 23. Start writing down the names of specific companies where you see yourself working in the future. Using your career center and online resources, build it one company at a time.
- Go to the company website and research contact information for the employer. Cold-call to get more information if needed, following the pointers on pages 33–35.

- Determine what materials you need to apply for the internship. Do you need a resume, cover letter, letters of recommendation, or writing samples? Write this on your Intern Queen Dream List.
- On your dream list, make note of the internship deadline, date you send out your application, and the date you plan to follow up.
- Create a calendar system for yourself. Read over the bulleted list of dates you should mark in your calendar.

Many people *talk* about getting internships. But what are they actually doing to find and land an opportunity? Following my guidance is going to take you from talking about getting internships to being a serious internship applicant with the potential to land any opportunity. I want to reiterate the importance of creating this list and organizing your application process. I cannot tell you the number of students that approach me and tell me they applied for internships and heard nothing back. When I ask them what they applied for, they don't remember. They didn't take the time to write down the information for each company and they didn't follow up. Take matters into your own hands and stay on top of your internship applications; it's the best way to gain control of the internship process.

I know the Intern Queen Dream List might seem like a simple concept—after all, it's just a list. But without this document, I would have been lost during my internship search. Take your time when creating your dream list and keep it updated, as this is your business plan and guidebook. The next chapter covers the tools you need to land the internship: your resume, cover letter, and letters of recommendation. If you organize your Intern Queen Dream List but send out useless materials, you have no chance of landing the internship. Continue reading to learn how to make your materials stand out from the rest of the pile. You'll be one step closer to your dream internship!

## CHAPTER 3

# Make Over
# **Your Tools**

You want an internship and an employer wants an intern. How do you connect? How do you get what *you* want and the employer get what *he or she* wants? Unfortunately you can't knock on the door or just call the employer up and say, "Hey, give me the internship." You must have clear, professional, and polished materials that can represent you on paper. These materials must capture the employer's attention and convince him or her to schedule an interview—because it's at the interview where you can sell yourself. As I explained in chapter 1, I've seen many new trends within the internship space, but the resume hasn't changed very much. The only change I've seen consistently is that resumes and cover letters are rarely sent through regular mail—everything is emailed. You email the majority of your applications, but you still need hard copies of your resume and cover letter for career fairs and interviews.

Today most internships require a resume and cover letter. My rule is to always send a cover letter, even if it's not requested. Cover letters help paint the picture for the employer. In this chapter, we dive right into how to create the perfect materials for your internship. If you've never created a resume, do not worry; I'm going to walk you through the entire process. The same thing goes for the cover letter. If you do have an existing resume or cover letter, take it out, and I'll help you give it a makeover. I created the Intern Queen Resume and Cover Letter Tools to help you learn how to organize your information and understand *what* goes *where*. Additionally I'll discuss creating letters of recommendation, student business cards, portfolios, and writing samples. Remember to always have a friend, parent, professor, or someone at your career center look over your materials before you submit them. It's always good to have a second set of eyes to make sure you haven't missed any spelling or grammatical errors.

# RESUMES

First, let's discuss the resumes I call "trash can resumes." A trash can resume has one or more of the following traits:

- Is more than one page long
- Includes an objective statement obviously written for another internship or job
- Says "Text me"
- Includes no contact information
- Includes no education information
- Is not formatted properly
- Has a photo or is printed out in colored ink
- Lacks student's name and email address
- Is not in chronological order

To help you format the *right* kind of resume, I've created the template on the opposite page to help you organize your information.

Read the information on each section of the resume below and then use the chart to complete your own resume. Remember, when filling out this information to leave a space between each section on your resume.

## Contact Information

Your name goes on the top of the resume, the very top. You can add your middle name or middle initial if you choose. Bold your name and make it one or two font sizes bigger than the rest of your resume to make it stand

| INTERN QUEEN RESUME TOOL |
|---|
| **Name (first and last)** |
| Address |
| Cell Phone Number |
| Email Address |
| **Education** |
| College/University You Currently Attend |
| School City/State |
| Expected Graduation (Month, Year) |
| Major: |
| Minor: |
| **Previous Experience** |
| Company Name/Years Spent at Company |
| Company Location |
| Title at Company |
| Description of Duties |
| |
| Company Name/Years Spent at Company |
| Company Location |
| Title at Company |
| Description of Duties |
| |
| *References Available Upon Request |

out. Under your name, list your address, your cell phone number, and your email address. You need to include your area code. Most students list their cell phone number. Recently I've seen resumes that say, "Please, text me." This is not acceptable.

Now, I have to stop here and remind you to create a professional email address. You can use your school email address if you'd like, but I suggest signing up for Gmail and creating a free professional email that you can use for years to come. People aren't going to be emailing your college address forever. Growing up, my AOL screen name was PrincessL84@aol.com. This was fine for instant messaging, but not for professional correspondence. The proper Gmail account for me was lauren.berger@gmail.com or lberger@gmail.com. My current email is lauren@internqueen.com. That's right, if you are reading this section—you now have my personal email address. We'll see how many of you take advantage of it!

If your parents live in the city where your internship is located, use their address, as it will help capture the employer's attention. Oftentimes employers do not understand why a student at Syracuse is applying to an internship in Los Angeles. Sadly they might throw the resume away if this is unclear. If you do have an address in the city where you would like to intern, I suggest using that. If you do not have an address in the city where you will be interning, explain your availability and the dates you plan on being in the internship location in your cover letter. If you are moving anytime soon, use a parent's permanent address. Again, use the cover letter to clearly explain when you will be in the internship destination.

## Education

The Education section can be listed underneath your contact information or at the bottom of the resume. For positions in certain fields that rely heavily on previous experience rather than schooling (such as communications—marketing, public relations, entertainment, or journalism), I would move the education information to the bottom. Your education section should include the full name of your college or university, city and state where your school is located, your major, your minor (if you have one—I didn't declare a minor), and your expected graduation date. This expected graduation date is key. Employers' eyes often go directly to this information as many have policies where they can only accept students currently enrolled in school. They want to make sure that when you intern, you will not have graduated already. You only need to list the month and the year of your expected graduation. If you are a high school student, include the name of your school, the years you've attended, and your expected graduation date. If you've already been accepted into a college, you can list that under Education. Next to the college, list the month and year that you will start.

If your GPA is required, list it in the Education section of your resume under your Expected Graduation Date. Most finance, engineering, and business internships require GPAs to be listed. The majority of communication-based employers do not ask for GPAs. Ross Herosian, internship director at Sirius XM Radio says, "Everything on a resume should have a strategic and beneficial reason for being there. If a student decides they want to have their GPA listed, it better be above a 3.5. Making a conscious decision to include this means that it better differentiate you from the pack or show an employer that this is something special or elite."[1]

## Previous Experience

Internships and jobs get listed under previous experience. List any internships and jobs in chronological order from the most recent to the least recent on your resume. (If you were fired from a job or internship, do not list it on your resume.) You'll need to mention the full company name, company location, and years you spent at the company. When you list the time spent at each company, list the month and year you started and the month and year you left. Also include a small paragraph or a bulleted list of tasks you accomplished during the span of that internship. You can list several previous jobs or internships but remember, if the resume is more than one page, it goes in the trash! Tailor your resume for the position to which you are applying. If you do not have any job or internship experience, that's when you start to pull from extracurricular activities and relevant coursework.

When it comes to irrelevant part-time jobs, think outside the box. Employers want to know that you are responsible and that others rely on you to accomplish something. Employers usually don't care *what* your job is, they care that you've held a job. My second job in high school was at Red Lobster in Clearwater, Florida. I listed my job description in a bulleted list: *customer service, customer satisfaction, greeting, managing team of hostesses, promotions.* You can always come up with something relevant that you've learned.

## References

At the bottom of your resume, include the following:

*References are available upon request.*

If references are required, you can best utilize the limited space by only including the actual names, emails, and contact numbers for references. I speak about references in the next chapter.

## Optional Skills Section

If you feel that you don't have enough previous or relevant experience on your resume, consider adding a skills section. I also suggest adding a skills section if you are applying for an internship that is computer or software heavy. For example, if you are applying for a graphic design internship, you should include a skills section that lists the names of the programs you are familiar with. If you are fluent in another language, you can also include that under the skills section. Your skills section can go under your contact information or at the end of the resume.

# RESUME CHECKLIST

Once you have a template for your personal resume, go through the following checklist, step by step, to be certain your resume is in great shape.

☑ Step 1: Presentation Check

An employer looks over your resume once, and only for a few seconds or minutes—we want it perfect!

### COLOR
Remember the movie *Legally Blonde*? In it, Elle Woods applies to Harvard Law with a hot pink resume sprayed with scented perfume. Don't do this—it may have been endearing and funny in the movie,

but your prospective employers won't think so. Keep your resume on a white background when emailing it to an employer. For hard-copy resumes, go to an office supply store and pick up a thick cream-colored paper and print your resume. It stands out from a pile but still looks professional. The only exception is if an employer tells you to be creative with your resume. An example of this might be a graphic design internship, art production internship, or even a social media internship.

### FONT

The standard font style for your resume is Times New Roman, size ten or twelve point. Use the bold function on your name and all of your section titles (education, previous experience, skills). You can also put your position titles in italics. Your name and the section titles can be two to four points larger than the rest of your resume.

### PHOTOS

Don't use pictures on your resume. An internship is not an audition. The idea is to get hired based on your professional qualifications and not on your looks.

### CONSISTENCY

Look over your spacing, capitalization, tenses, years, locations, and bullets. All of these need to be consistent throughout your resume. Make sure you have the same amount of spacing between sections and lines of the resume.

### LENGTH

Students have problems keeping their resumes down to one page. They want to include everything they've ever done on their resume. Even though I've had fifteen internships, my resume is still only one page. If I applied for an entertainment internship, I included my relevant entertainment experience. If I applied for a journalism opportunity, I would include my writing experience. No matter how much experience you've had, keep your resume to one page. We will speak more about how to tailor your resume in Step 4, the Relevancy Test.

☑ Step 2: Objective

First, let me say that you don't need an objective on your resume. However, if you are applying to intern or work for a company with several different departments promoting open positions, you might include an objective statement to distinguish exactly which position you are applying for. Also, if you're overqualified for a position, include an objective statement. An example of an objective for a business marketing internship at LinkedIn could read like this: "Obtain a summer business marketing internship with LinkedIn where I can learn about the industry, gain experience, and bring creativity to the position."

Make sure that your objective is NOT any of the following:

- A long and wordy statement that looks like you are trying to show off your vocabulary rather than get to the point
- A statement that says you are looking for a *job* on an internship application or vice versa
- An objective that has nothing to do with the position you are applying for
- A generic objective that looks like you've applied for ten different internships with the same line

☑ Step 3: Content

Make sure that you clearly indicate the following information on your resume:

- First and last name
- Current address
- Phone number
- Email address
- Education
- GPA (if required)
- Previous experience

☑ Step 4. Relevancy Test

I graduated from college in 2006 and needed a job. Los Angeles called my name, and I went running weeks after graduation. My internship contacts helped me land an interview at Creative Artists Agency (CAA), the largest talent agency in the world. I needed to submit a resume but knew it could only be one page. At this point, I'd completed fifteen internships throughout college. I couldn't list all of them on my resume. My entertainment experience was at a variety of local and national companies. You must think *bragging rights*. Out of my list of entertainment experience, what was the most impressive? In my case, that was FOX, MTV, and NBC, so that's what I listed on my resume for CAA.

Now, if I had no entertainment experience, I would have put my public relations experience on the resume since I dealt with media-related companies. If I had no internship experience, I would have listed some of my relevant entertainment and communications-based coursework. I also would have listed any clubs or organizations and described in detail what my responsibilities were for each one.

To wrap up this section, I've included an example of a great resume on the following page. One of my Intern Queen Campus Ambassadors, Alicia, who attends Towson University, used this resume to successfully land her dream public relations internship.[2]

# COVER LETTERS

Imagine this: You are a New York City magazine editor and looking for the best crop of interns for summer. You receive a stack of eight hundred applications for your position. Some of the applicants send both resumes and cover letters and others only send resumes. You are flipping through the large stack, exhausted and you see a resume from a student at the University of Minnesota. No cover letter is attached. As an employer with 799 other applications to look at and no real information on this University of Minnesota student, when she plans to come to the city, or if she applied for the correct position—why would you call that candidate back? You need the cover letter to tie things together and reference the employers so they know you are truly interested in their position.

That's right, the cover letter needs to do two things: tie things together and reference the employer. First off, *tying it together* means putting your individual scenario in perspective for the employer. Employers must identify what position you are applying for, where you go to school, what year you graduate, your major, when you will be available, if you are interning

# Alicia Valko

12 Street Road, Apt. 2, Towson, MD 21204     avalko1@email.com     (555) 555-5555

**Education**

**Towson University (Towson, MD)**     August 2009 to Present
Major: Public Relations/Advertising
Minor: Italian
Expected graduation: May 2013
GPA: 3.6

**Previous Experience**

**Jack Morton Worldwide (New York, NY)**     June 2011 – August 2011
**Strategy Intern**
- Added value to the Jack Morton team by conducting market research and competitive brand analysis, consulting with clients on social media execution, and assisting with RFP completion
- Positioned myself as a thought leader in the brand experience space by contributing my insight and perspective to the award-winning "Jack: Experience Brands" blog, which reaches over 1,300 subscribers
- Developed competencies in digital, consumer engagement, and stakeholder alignment

**MGH Modern Marketing (Baltimore, MD)**     February 2011 – May 2011
**Public Relations Intern**
- Created, distributed, and followed up on news materials, including: press releases, calendar listings, media advisories, fact sheets, and media kits
- Built and maintained media contacts and mentions lists
- Generated content for clients' social media messaging to engage core audiences

**Mercer Regional Chamber of Commerce (Hamilton, NJ)**
**Public Relations Intern**     May 2010 – August 2010
- Drafted press releases; compiled press lists and media contact information
- Facilitated member networking events

**Jack Morton Exhibits (Princeton, NJ)**     June 2010 – August 2010
**Project Management Intern**
- Participated in the "I Love My Brand" business development initiative
- Assisted with the fabrication of tradeshow exhibits for Fortune 500 clients
- Supported the project management team by preparing client presentations, assembling exhibitor information packets, and organizing travel itineraries
- Presented senior management with business solutions and expansion opportunities

**Princeton Communications Group (Trenton, NJ)**     February 2009 – June 2009
**Advertising Intern**
- Drafted press releases for various consumer and health care clients
- Collaborated on radio commercials, annual reports, and ad concepts and headlines

**Related Experience**

**Central Atlantic Affiliate of College and University Residence Halls (CAACURH) Conference Team (Towson, MD)**
**Public Relations / Sponsorship Chair**     January 2010 – Present
- Communicate with local businesses to create relationships with potential sponsors
- Collaborate with other committee members to plan and host a conference attended by over 500 student leaders in the Central Atlantic region

**Intern Queen, www.internqueen.com**     November 2010 – Present
**Campus Ambassador**
- Serve as a liaison between the Intern Queen and Towson University communities
- Contribute blog posts to "I Am Intern" blog, with emphasis on personal branding

**Towson University (Towson, MD)**     February 2011 – Present
**Resident Assistant**
- Develop and maintain relationships with over 40 residents
- Assess the social and educational needs and interests of residents and present quality programs that meet those needs
- Communicate and enforce Housing and Residence Life policies

**CV-Blogger, www.cv-blogger.co.uk**     October 2010 – December 2010
**Guest Blogger**
- Contributed guest blog posts to CV-Blogger site
- Informed readers about trends in job searching, with emphasis on social media use

*References are available upon request.

through a special program, and your career goals by looking over the cover letter.

The second concept is *referencing the employer*. How are you going to hold the attention of the person reading your resume? The answer is by constantly bringing everything back to the employer. The employer's attention is held by mentioning his or her name in your customized materials and constantly drawing parallels between your experience and the company.

## Intern Queen's Cover Letter

Remember, this is a quick guide on how to create a cover letter if you want to write up a new one or revamp an old version. Follow my advice and you will put something great together in no time!

### HEADER
Remember when you learned to write a business letter in elementary school? It is time to put that knowledge to good use. You need to have the full date written out at the top of the paper, the company's name and address, and your address. Also, include your phone number and email under your address so the person knows how to contact you.

### OPENING
The old school cover letter opening "To Whom This May Concern" comes across too generic for a cover letter. If you do not know who you are sending the cover letter to at the company, at least address it to the company, for example, "To *Marie Claire* magazine." The other option is to use "Dear Internship Coordinator," which is also okay. You can use "To" or "Dear"— this is just a preference of style. If you do find a contact person at the company, address it to the person's first and last name. For example, if you were sending me a cover letter it would read "Lauren Berger" or "Ms. Berger."

### PARAGRAPH 1
Explain who you are, the exact opportunity you are applying for, and your availability, especially if it's an out-of-state opportunity. Of course, you'll

want to include where you go to school, your major, minor, expected graduation date, and your current year in school.

## PARAGRAPH 2
Talk about your best professional experience (from your resume) and how those experiences make you the best candidate for the position. You must tie everything back to the employer. Always think, what do I bring to the table and how does that relate to what the company is looking for? This is a chance for you to show off your skill set and your knowledge of the company. Remember, you are bragging here. Use the most impressive, relevant experience from your resume to show off your skills.

## PARAGRAPH 3
Use this last paragraph to talk up your personality traits that make you right for the position. Don't forget to thank the employer for his or her time. Always end with something like

Thank you for your time and consideration. I look forward to hearing from you.

## CLOSING
The closing of the letter should be signed "Best, "Best Regards," or "Sincerely." Make sure to write both your first and last name.

# A Few Cover Letter Do's and Don'ts

Once you create or have a template for your cover letter, review the sections below. They'll help you understand what to do and not do in your cover letter.

### DON'T WRITE AN OBVIOUSLY GENERIC COVER LETTER.
If I can tell that you are sending the same cover letter to every potential employer, I'm likely to hit the delete button. I want to read a cover letter that tells me you know exactly what position you are applying for and what my company does. You must hold my attention. Don't just speak of yourself and your personal and professional capabilities but also tie them into my

company and how they will benefit me. Your cover letter should be carefully customized and crafted to catch the employer's eye.

## DO INCLUDE INFORMATION ON LOGISTICS

When applicable, a cover letter needs to explain logistics. For example, when I was a student at University of Central Florida in Orlando, I wanted to go to Los Angeles for a summer out-of-state internship. It was my job to answer the following questions when writing my cover letter:

- When was I planning to be in Los Angeles?
- What dates was I planning on being in Los Angeles?
- What day could I start?

Students should state *when* they are planning to be in the internship location. Employers don't want to waste their time contacting applicants who *might* be in the city. If you are only going to be in that location depending on the internship—fake it. You may never get a call back if the employer doesn't take your interest seriously.

## DO BE CERTAIN ALL INFORMATION IS CORRECT

Any resume or cover letter with wrong information goes right into the trash. If I receive an application for Warner Brothers Television but the cover letter reads NBC Universal, I'll trash it. Attention to detail is crucial.

## DO KEEP YOUR FOCUS ON THE INTERNSHIP

I also don't like to read cover letters for internships that speak about getting a full-time job. Internship applications and job applications are two different things and should be handled separately.

## DON'T WRITE A NOVEL

On Tuesdays, I run #internchat on Twitter. It's an open platform for students to directly communicate with me. They can ask me any internship question. I've been doing #internchat for more than a year, and almost every week I'm asked about a cover letter and how long it should be. My answer is always the same: "One page." Your cover letter needs to be three concise, to-the-point paragraphs that fit within the standard margins of one page. If the cover letter is longer, it starts looking like a novel and employers may elect to delete it.

## DO CONNECT THE DOTS FOR THE EMPLOYER

I cannot emphasize this enough: you must connect the dots for the employer. Meghan was an art history major at the University of Florida. Upon graduation, Meghan looked at her job options. She stopped by Target's booth at a career fair and learned about their management training programs. It turns out that Target is one of the best companies to work for in terms of benefits and how they treat their employees. Meghan was interested. But she wasn't a hospitality or management major like several of the other management training program candidates. She addressed this in her cover letter. She indicated that yes, she was an art history major, but because of the great opportunity that Target provided their employees, the benefits, the team-leading opportunities—she was interested. She connected the dots for the employer so they didn't make assumptions of their own. Meghan ended up landing a job in management at Target. She still enjoys art history but is happy with her decision to work for Target.

Here is an example of a great cover letter from former Intern Queen Campus Ambassador Andrea.[3] This is the cover letter she used to land a win-ternship with *Marie Claire* magazine. I like how Andrea connects the dots for the employer and explains her specific situation. In this case, Andrea explains the quarter system at Ohio University, and she points to her specific experience that makes her the right person for the job. She keeps it short, sweet, and to-the-point. Andrea landed the internship.

# LETTERS OF RECOMMENDATION

In chapter 1, I spoke about the reasons to take internships and explained that networking and building relationships are essential. You can determine if a professional would go to bat for you by asking yourself, "Would he or

Andrea R. Teggart
1 Holly Road
Athens, Ohio 45701
(555) 555-5555

September 4, 2011

Marie Claire
300 West 57th Street, 34th Floor
New York, NY 10019-1497

Dear Internship Coordinator:

After learning about the fashion department opportunity at *Marie Claire* and evaluating my various experiences as a journalism and retail merchandising student, I am very interested in interning for your company. I am currently a college senior at Ohio University in Athens, Ohio, and I would like to intern at *Marie Claire* this winter. Ohio University's academic calendar is different from most schools in that we are on the quarter system, rather than semesters. We have a seven-week winter break from mid-November to early January and I would love to intern during this time period or during winter quarter from early January to early April.

I know that I would be a strong addition to the *Marie Claire* team as a fashion department intern. I'm confident in my ability to communicate effectively, research, use several media monitoring programs, and stay up-to-date on this fast-paced industry. I will also bring retail merchandising knowledge and experience to the table. My retail merchandising classes inspired me to help start an online fashion magazine at Ohio University. *Thread Magazine* (www.outhreadmag.com) is a full-feature, student-produced fashion magazine and my involvement has created my interest in a finding a job in the fashion industry after graduation. Being involved with *Thread* has also taught me the "ins and outs" of how a magazine is run effectively and smoothly. Aside from professional qualities, I will bring a fresh personality to *Marie Claire* to contribute unique ideas, plans, and visions that are necessary for team brainstorming and campaigning for magazine photo shoots, story boards, and more.

I have also enclosed my resume with this cover letter and would be more than willing to put you in contact with references from other internships or from my university. I look forward to hearing from you about this opportunity in the near future. Thank you for your time and consideration.

Sincerely,

*Andrea Teggart*

Andrea R. Teggart

she write me a letter of recommendation?" If the answer is yes, you have been successful. Build relationships with contacts who will write these letters for you. A great letter of recommendation speaks to your professional characteristics from a personal standpoint. Everyone needs three letters of recommendation; an academic one from a professor, a professional one from an employer, and a character reference from a personal contact. You can never have too many recommendations. After each semester, identify one professor with whom you have a relationship and who can speak to your good grades and work ethic. Ask that professor to write you a letter of recommendation.

At Florida State, I needed a letter of recommendation after my sophomore year of college for an internship application. I didn't have relationships with any of my professors, so I went to visit an archeology professor from freshman year. He barely remembered me and we had an extremely awkward conversation where I asked if he could write me a letter of recommendation. He wrote the letter, but it was generic and short—if he hardly remembered me how could I expect him to rave about me in a letter? Build relationships with your professors. Ask them questions. Let them know you want to excel in your class and you care about your grades. It will pay off.

The professional letters of recommendation come from employers or internship coordinators. After completing any job or internship, always ask for a letter of recommendation two weeks before your final day at the company. These executives maintain busy schedules and it's difficult to pin them down once you've already left the company. I'll discuss in more detail how to approach them in chapter 9.

Family friends or relatives can write you character references that speak of your personality and character traits. Team coaches or group supervisors can also write these character references for you.

My Intern Queen secret tip regarding letters of recommendation is to help out your employer by providing a detailed list of accomplishments from your internship. Here's what I did:

During my internship at BWR Public Relations, I worked for a great executive, Eric. At the end of my internship, Eric offered me a job, but I declined as I wanted to return to school in the fall. I did, however, need a letter of recommendation and knew that Eric's schedule was extremely busy.

I remember nervously knocking on Eric's door one afternoon. Eric made it clear that he liked my work, but I knew he was busy and didn't want him to get upset that I was asking him to write a letter of recommendation. I knew his day usually slowed down after lunch because New York calls were done for the day with the time difference. I poked my head in his door and said,

"Hi, Eric. I know you are really busy right now and I wanted to request a letter of recommendation before the end of my internship. I can make you a list of some things it could include if that will save you time . . ." He looked at me and paused for a moment, "Great, Lauren. Just put it on my desk to look over tomorrow afternoon."

Done and done: I wrote down a list of the five most impressive things I'd done at my internship. I printed the list out and gave it to Eric. He looked it over, put it in letter format, printed it out on company letterhead, and signed it. I now had a stand-out letter from an impressive executive at a very high-profile PR Firm. You want to have a letter that stands out from the rest and doesn't come off as generic or as one of hundreds of the same letter. Often professors run into this issue because they have literally hundreds of letters to write. Use my technique when you can. There are exceptions to this rule. You *will* find bosses and executives who want to write you great letters. When you are in that situation, take advantage of it!

Below are a few tips to remember when asking employers for letters of recommendation:

- Employers, professors, or friends who write letters of recommendation for you should address them "To Whom This May Concern," unless you are having them write the letter for a specific opportunity for which you are applying. In that case, they should use the person's first and last name. The letter should be dated. Letters are considered out-of-date after a one year.
- Letters of recommendation should be on company letterhead or school letterhead. They should also have the real signature from the person who wrote them.

- As soon as you get a letter, make ten photocopies of it. Keep these in a safe place and put them in clear plastic sleeves (that you can buy at the office supply store) so they stay fresh and clean. Normally you can submit photocopied letters with internship applications unless the application specifies the original copy.
- Bring a portfolio with you to interviews. I will discuss this further in chapter 5. Keep these letters in your portfolio just in case you are asked for them on the spot.

# THE EXTRAS

Today additional items get sent along with resumes, cover letters, and letters of recommendation. I call them *the extras*: writing samples, business cards, online portfolios, and hard-copy portfolios. The materials requested depend on the nature of the business. Media companies that feature magazine or publishing internships often require writing samples and ask students to come to the interview with a portfolio. Graphic design companies often require online portfolios. Employers do not want incomplete applications, so make sure to read over that list of required materials in the internship posting to make sure you send in everything necessary.

## Business Cards

Student business cards have become popular, so if you decide to make them, make them well. If I have a bunch of attractive looking cards in my hand and one "plain Jane" card, the plain card makes that student look lazy and gives the impression that the student didn't put in the effort. I recently spoke at a PRSSA (Public Relations Student Society of America) Conference in Washington, DC, and was impressed with two business cards that included personal designs and blog links (in addition to their basic information). Here is a list of what you must include on your student business card, and a sample of how it should be formatted:

- Your first and last names (middle initial optional)
- Email address
- Address
- Phone number
- Year in school (freshman, sophomore, junior, senior)
- Major
- Expected graduation date

*Julie R. Polman*

julie.polman@gmail.com
444 High Street, #3

Senior, Stanford College | English major
*Graduating June 17, 2012*

A great resource for business cards is your career center. Go in and ask if the school provides help with these. Most schools have cards available for discounted prices or even for free.

Career fairs, guest lectures, and interviews are the best times to pass out your student business cards. Don't be too aggressive or pushy with the cards. Ask the employers if you can give them a business card with your contact information on it, but don't shove it in their faces.

## Visual CVs/Portfolios

Many employers and industries require portfolios from students in order to get an interview. A portfolio is a collection of your work, whether it be in the form of writing, art work, photography, or design work. Publishing, architecture, design, graphic design, marketing, public relations, journalism, and photography internships frequently require portfolios (hard copy or electronic) from potential applicants. Have both formats available so you can submit according to an employer's preference.

VisualCV (www.visualcv.com) is an online program and website that helps you organize an online portfolio, or visual CV (short for curriculum vitae). The site generates a link for you to send to employers so they can easily browse through your work. For hard-copy portfolios, head to your office supply store and get a binder with laminated inserts that you can add to when you fill up the ones allotted in the book. Always keep back-up copies of the work in your portfolio and, of course, scan it all so you have online versions. Employers skim these quickly, so put your best work in the front of the portfolio.

## Writing Samples

Writing samples stand alone or can be presented within a portfolio. Normally these are required from employers who plan on publishing your work or having you proofread others' work—magazines, publishing companies, literary agencies, blogs, and websites.

When selecting writing samples to submit, consider the following:

- Customize your collection of writing samples. Think about the company to which you are submitting. CollegeCandy.com is a popular blog about the college experience. If you were submitting a writing sample to them, it should be something they could imagine on their site. I recommend you stay away from a school essay in this case and try to find a shorter article on a lighter topic to highlight your voice. The employer should read your sample and be confident that your writing and style is a match for the site—and, therefore, you're a great match for the internship.
- Writing samples should be no longer than one page each. If they look like novels, the employer is less likely to read them.
- Your work should not contain any grammatical errors. Have a friend or professor proofread your work before you submit. Make sure you run spell-check!

- You may submit a school essay if you feel it demonstrates your voice.
- Unless you were told to include an edgy essay, avoid submitting work that comes across as aggressive or gives a big push to anything political, sexual, or religious. An employer doesn't need to know your religious views, sexual orientation, or political party preference before you start your internship.
- Don't submit work with curse words, unless it's within the context of a script or screenplay. Don't give your employer a reason to doubt your professionalism.
- Make sure you submit a document that's in its final version and doesn't have tracked changes all over it.
- If writing samples are needed for the application, number each one, and attach them along with your resume and cover letter. Save your files and label them with your first and last name and the corresponding number if you are sending more than one sample. They should all have professional titles. The employer wants everything in one place and doesn't want scattered applications. You should also include the writing samples in your portfolio printed on either regular computer paper or a thick, light-colored paper purchased from an office supply store.

I speak about blogging and how to submit blogs to employers in chapter 4 on social media.

## ♛ INTERN QUEEN CHAPTER ESSENTIALS

- Block out time to work on your materials.
- Have your Intern Queen Dream List in front of you to easily customize your materials.
- If you already have drafts of resumes and cover letters, print them out and have them in front of you to take notes.
- If you don't have a resume, use the Intern Queen Resume Tool to help jot down ideas and format your resume.

- Read over the tips provided for resumes, cover letters, and letters of recommendation. Make notes on your current materials as needed.
- If you decide to make a portfolio or student business cards, speak to your career center about free or discount resources on campus.
- If you need to buy a portfolio folder or business cards, find deals online first and then head out to the office supply stores.
- Save clean hard copies of your files.
- Print out at least ten copies of your resume and put them in your car or in the bag that you take to school so you always have a copy on you. If someone asks for your resume on the spot, you don't want to miss out on the opportunity.

Remember, even if you don't have relevant experience, you can still create meaningful materials that represent you well. How will your personal and professional attributes serve as an asset to the company? Once you look over these tips and examples, I'm confident you can go back to your dream list and start sending applications. Take each application seriously and take the time to customize each one. You might be the most qualified and capable student on the planet, but if your materials don't state that, you could miss out on the opportunity.

Don't continue onto the next chapter until you get your materials in order. Make notes, revise, cut things out—but most importantly get it done, as this is a pivotal part of the internship search process.

After you put time and effort into your Intern Queen Dream List and creating customized resumes and cover letters, it will be time for you to turn your attention to social media. In chapter 4, I'll explain not only how social media can harm you during the internship process but also how it can help you land a position.

## CHAPTER 4

# Monitor Your
# **Social Media**

My brand succeeds on a daily basis because of social media and the influence of websites like Facebook, Twitter, and LinkedIn. My audience knows of www.internqueen.com thanks to blogs, tweets, and Facebook "likes." Fifteen percent of the students that visit my site come from a combination of Facebook and Twitter. I'm convinced that social networks are just as helpful in helping students define their personal brand and find internship and job opportunities.

Let's examine this concept further. Social networks help me grow my professional brand and connect with my audience. It's up to me, the owner of my brand, to monitor what information I put out to my networks. As an intern and soon-to-be professional, *you* want to grow your brand, connect with target employers, and monitor what you put out into the universe. In this chapter, we explore personal branding and how to properly monitor and utilize social networks like Facebook, Twitter, and LinkedIn to land internships. In the first section, I break down each network and review how to protect your image and properly create profiles on each site. I'll also discuss some time management techniques so you don't find yourself spending all of your time online. Afterward I explain how to connect with target employers on these networks, monitor the information they put out, and utilize the information in your internship search. I end the chapter with a section on blogging, explaining how to blog and how to spread the word about your work. By the end, you will feel in control of your personal brand, online presence, and ability to connect with employers using social media. Remember, this is about protecting and utilizing the most important brand in your life: YOU!

# CREATING YOUR PERSONAL BRAND

Personal branding doesn't mean you need to call yourself Top Chef, Dr. Love, or even the Intern Queen; it means creating a voice for yourself. Three great tools to help develop your brand are Facebook, Twitter, and LinkedIn—these networks help you find your voice and promote your work to a massive and seemingly infinite audience. I spoke to Dan Schawbel, author of *Me 2.0: 4 Steps to Building Your Future*, about how students can find their personal brand. Schawbel says, "Personal branding is the process by which we figure out what makes us special and then start communicating it, through various media, to the right audience. For students, this means that you need to figure out what you want to do with your career, put yourself and your ideas out on the Internet through a blog and social network profiles, and then network with employers directly online and offline. The sooner you start networking, gaining new skills, and becoming an active participant in online communities, the easier it will be to get an internship and a job when you graduate. A personal brand is built through hard work, determination and the support of your friends, family, and the rest of your network. Be true to yourself, stay authentic, and invest time in your career if you want to get something out of it."[1]

Ask yourself the following questions when thinking about your personal brand:

- What image do I want to project to employers?
- What am I passionate about?
- What do I have strong opinions about?

At www.internqueen.com, I have a team of Intern Queen Campus Ambassadors from colleges and universities worldwide who help spread the Intern Queen brand around their campuses. One of my campus ambassadors, Chandra, from Florida State University, does an excellent job of branding herself. Chandra's blog is www.fsufashiongirl.com and her twitter handle is @FSUFashionGirl. She is interested in the fashion industry and her goal is to work for a fashion company in New York City. Chandra's advice to other students who want to brand themselves is this: "Brand yourself not only for the job you want but also for what you are passionate about. I tend to follow people on Twitter and Facebook who are passionate and knowledgeable about their field. The most important yet hardest thing to do is to find your voice. Once you find it, stick with it. People will grow to love it!"[2]

Now, not everyone is as lucky as Chandra and knows exactly what they want to do. If you are still weighing your options, follow my advice from chapter 1 and write down a list of your dream companies. Start researching the companies from your dream list and see if they have social media profiles—this is the best way to start. Let's say you are an accounting student—a great Twitter handle to follow is Ernst and Young (www.twitter.com/ernst_and_young). Or maybe your dream job is with a company like Geico (www.twitter.com/geicocareers), which puts out great career advice and company information on a consistent basis.

In the following sections, I will take you through each social network, explaining how to monitor them and use them to your advantage.

## Using Facebook

Michael called me up in 2005. He was a close friend from my first out-of-state internship with *Backstage* newspaper in New York. He wanted to connect and stay in touch through a website called Facebook. I had no idea what he was talking about. Michael attended American University, and Facebook was something people at his school were hooked on. A few months later, University of Central Florida started buzzing about the same site. I signed up and put together my profile. Facebook ignited across the country. My friends and I obsessed over the site and updated our profiles constantly. Facebook developed picture uploading capabilities and became the way to show friends what you were up to. Typical Facebook behavior included making sure your profile picture looked as glamorous as possible without being an actual glamor shot. When pictures came out well, the common phrase was "Facebook worthy."

I used Facebook to connect with friends from high school and summer camp as well as current classmates. Facebook users provided a college email address to register for the site. That placed boundaries on the types of relationships I was maintaining through Facebook. As the site grew, Facebook stopped requiring college email addresses to join. Eventually everyone joined. My fifteen-year-old cousin joined and requested my friendship. My best friend's father joined along with my first boss from Creative Artist Agency. The Facebook dilemma of how much is too much started to circulate. The social network that existed solely to connect college friends was now open to the world. Just as a conversation between friends changes when a parent walks in the room, my conversation on Facebook and the information I was sharing needed to be tweaked. Pictures displaying drunken nights, funny faces, and photos that could be interpreted the wrong way had to be taken down.

I currently have 1,415 friends on Facebook. And yes, I actually know 99 percent of these people. If I were to gauge who the most active Facebook users out of my friends are, I'd have to say my *parents'* friends and my *friends'* parents. Things have changed. According to Facebook, the site has over five hundred million users, and their largest growing demographic is people over the age of thirty-five.[3]

It's time to control the information you put out into the universe. Parents, professors, and potential employers *are* looking you up on Facebook and might be judging you by what they see. Most employers do not have a policy in place with regard to social media; however, employers are active on Facebook and if they have their Facebook tab open at work, it's very easy for them to type a potential candidate's name into the search bar. Students *do* get fired for inappropriate Facebook profiles. As an intern, you represent the brand and employer for which you intern. They view you as an extension of their company. And at the end of the day, how embarrassing would it be to get fired for an inappropriate Facebook photo or wall post? Make sure you are represented well online.

## MONITOR YOUR FACEBOOK PHOTOS

Go through *all* of your Facebook picture albums, tagged photos, and mobile uploads. Take this weekend to start going through these photos. Ask yourself, "Can I show this picture to my parents, grandparents, professors, and any potential employer at any time in my life?" If the answer is yes across the board, keep the photo or tag. If you are hesitant, save it to your computer, and click delete. You cannot risk your future for the sake of a Facebook photo—no matter how great you might look.

Amber is a close friend of mine who loves Facebook. She thinks she is the paparazzi when we go out. She posts 135 pictures on Facebook the morning after and tags everyone in them. Everyone has a friend like Amber. The good news is that we can all untag ourselves in photos and once we do, people like Amber cannot retag them. I've asked Amber to stop tagging me in random photographs on several occasions. Sometimes Amber remembers and other times she doesn't. It's not Amber's responsibility. It's mine. Monitor what goes online.

In situations like this, speak with your friend and address the issue of posting inappropriate pictures online. The best way to do this is one-on-one without others around. Explain that potential employers might come across the photos and you don't want your professional contacts to see the personal photos. Warning! This might be a slightly awkward conversation, but I promise it's worth it.

## MONITOR YOUR FACEBOOK PROFILE

I spoke at Wabash College a few weeks back. The conversation turned to social media. A middle-aged man raised his hand in the back of the room— he worked for a luxury international car brand. "We are hiring interns. I had a stack of resumes on my desk last week. I and another team member looked each candidate up on Facebook. If we saw anything inappropriate, we didn't call them." To keep this from happening to you, consider the following tips.

- Put your profile settings on Private so that only your friends can see your photos, wall posts, and comments.
- Develop the everyone-knows-everyone mentality. Just because someone isn't your friend doesn't mean that person can't find someone who is friends with you and look at your profile.
- Don't friend just anyone on Facebook. That person might write inappropriate comments on your wall or try to hack into your account.
- Make sure your profile picture doesn't contain alcohol, drugs, funny faces, body parts that should be covered, or scandalous clothing.
- Don't include any foul language or jokes that could be misread on your actual Facebook profile.
- You don't need to write everything you are doing on Facebook. Limit the amount of information you provide to the public. Employers don't need to see your everyday whereabouts.

## MONITOR YOUR FACEBOOK WALL

Monitor your wall posts. Scroll through and make sure none of your friends have written curse words or anything about hooking up, smoking, drinking, or inside jokes that could be misread. Keep a constant watch over your wall and delete comments that don't sound right. Don't feel bad about deleting them; your future is more important than your friends' comments.

## DON'T LET FACEBOOK RULE YOUR LIFE

I have a confession. In the past, I've stayed up for hours on Facebook, stalking everyone I went to high school with—looking at their photos and browsing their lives. I started looking for old friends I hadn't seen in years and would get addicted to looking at random photos of people. I know that you have been there! The second I catch myself and actually realize what I'm doing, I leave the site. How many times has this happened to you? How many hours do you think you've wasted on Facebook? Facebook users spend a combined total of seven hundred billion minutes per month on Facebook, according to the website itself.[4] As interns, you are becoming professionals and must learn to monitor and value your time. In chapter 1, we discussed your calendar and managing multiple activities and commitments. I want to reiterate that time is the most valuable thing you have: don't waste it—especially on Facebook. Here are the rules I follow to make sure I'm not wasting time on Facebook:

- I allow myself ten to twenty minutes of personal time on my personal Facebook page each day. I usually wait until after work hours to do this. I suggest waiting until after your internship and schoolwork is done and then allowing yourself ten minutes to respond to messages, scroll through the feeds from the day, watch funny videos, check out the photos you were tagged in (make sure they are appropriate), and look at what your friends are up to. And then cut it off—you don't need to spend your time looking at what other people are doing. Focus on what *you* are doing.
- Download the Facebook application on your phone. If you always need to feel in the loop, check Facebook while in line at the grocery store or while you are waiting for an appointment. This way all of your free time at home doesn't need to be spent on the website.
- Enable the function under Settings that notifies you via email every time you are tagged in a photo. Remember, you must make sure those photos are appropriate. Try to do this from your phone so that you don't have your desktop browser open to Facebook. Once Facebook gets opened on your computer, it gets addicting and difficult to close.
- If you need to upload pictures, decide which night of the week you will do that, upload them, tag them as you wish, and be done with it. You don't need to check it every five seconds to see if friends commented; you will see that the following day during your Facebook time.

## Monitoring Twitter

Katie is a student from Dallas who is interested in the health care industry and who connected with a local insurance firm in Dallas over Twitter. They were direct messaging (DM'ing) back and forth about an internship opportunity and set up an interview time over Twitter. Katie forgot to write this in her calendar and missed the interview. The interview was at 9 a.m., and at 9 a.m. Katie tweeted, "grocery shopping suckas." Don't use words like "suckas" on Twitter. Because Katie and the employer initially connected over Twitter, there was a good chance that the employer saw this unprofessional tweet. You never know who follows you or has access to your profile, even if the settings are private. As it turns out, the employer did see Katie's tweet and left her the following not-so-nice phone message:

> Hi Katie,
> It seems that you were out running errands during the time of our interview. I just don't feel comfortable extending this opportunity to you as we must hire professional students. I don't feel your sense of professionalism has shined through in this instance. Best of luck in the future.

*Ouch.*

## THE TWITTER BASICS

Twitter is updated in real time, like Facebook. Twitter monitors *trending topics*, meaning the most popular names, places, people, subjects mentioned in tweets from all Twitter users. This provides a great source of news and information.

You've probably heard words like *tweet and tweeps* used by Twitter lovers. To help you navigate this Twitter lingo, I've included a few terms to help you better understand the *Twitterverse* (universe according to Twitter).

> *tweets/tweeting:* When an individual posts a status update to Twitter. Note: All of your followers can read your Tweets. If your Tweets are not set up to be private, the public can read your tweets.

> *direct message (DM):* This is the way one Twitter user sends a private message to another. You can only Direct Message people who follow you. This is like Facebook messaging.

> *ReTweet (RT or RT'd):* If someone uses the term RT, it stands for ReTweet. An RT means that you are repeating or retweeting what someone else has written on their status.

*tweeps:* The people you follow on Twitter and the people who follow you can be referred to as your *tweeps.*

*hashtag:* This refers to placing a # at the end of a tweet to help categorize what that tweet is about. You can use hashtags to create a stream about a certain topic. During #internchat, we hashtag every tweet with #internchat. If someone wants to follow our chat, he or she can just click on the hashtag and only see the tweets that have that hashtag. This helps to filter your tweets so interested tweeps can read one specific topic.

## SETTING UP A TWITTER PAGE

If you don't already have a Twitter account, go to twitter.com and click Sign Up to create a username. Just like with Facebook, your profile picture needs to be appropriate. Twitter limits the amount of information you provide about yourself. It's not nearly as in-depth as a Facebook profile. If you blog or have a website, include this link in the *Bio* section.

## CREATING STATUS UPDATES

What would you write on your Facebook status? Start by putting the same type of information on Twitter. Once your friends start to follow you on Twitter, they can get updates about your day. If you read an interesting article, put the link on Twitter. My Twitter name is @internqueen (www .twitter.com/internqueen). Normally, my tweets are about internship listings, but I like to mix it up. Here are some examples of the types of tweets I send out:

@internqueen: Great PR opportunity at company in Los Angeles—click here for more details! www.internqueen.com
@internqueen: Hey, interns! What did you learn from your internship this week?
@internqueen: Rocking out to the Intern Queen Official Playlist on YouTube! Love these songs.
@internqueen: Always send a cover letter—even when the employer does not request one!

## DECIDING WHO TO FOLLOW

Keep the number of people you follow to under three hundred so it's manageable. You don't need to follow everyone who follows you. I made that mistake when I first started using Twitter. Follow a mixture of friends, people you admire, favorite celebrities, and target employers. At the end of the chapter, I will discuss how to find target employers on Twitter.

Use the Twitter List function to organize who you follow. The List function can be found directly under any user's profile picture. As soon as you follow someone, add them to one of your lists. You can name the list anything you want. Let's say you start a list called "favorite celebs." You determine if that list is private (only you can see it) or public (anyone that looks you up on Twitter can see it). If you already use Twitter, sort the tweeps you follow into lists to make the most of Twitter and keep up with the people who interest you the most.

## WATCH THE TIME YOU SPEND TWEETING

Frequently I hear about students landing opportunities because of interactions over Twitter. (I'll explain how to use social media for this purpose later in this chapter). At the beginning, update your status once per day when you have something you really want to say. Download the Twitter mobile app on your phone so that you can update on the go and you don't have to spend time at your regular computer on Twitter. Popular mobile applications for Twitter include Tweetberry and UberTweet. Again, using the *Twitter List* functionality saves you time and energy on Twitter as you can segment the feeds you read. Like Facebook, Twitter can become addictive, so give yourself a ten-minute-per-day limit on the network.

## Utilizing LinkedIn

Monika, one of my Intern Queen Campus Ambassadors, attends Rutgers University and is traveling to South Korea to study abroad. She wants to conduct informational interviews while in South Korea to learn more about the human resources industry. Monika uses LinkedIn and decided to look up Hyundai-Kia, one of the largest companies based in South Korea. Her search returned hundreds of people employed by Hyundai-Kia. LinkedIn indexes the search results by way of *shared connections*, meaning that if any of the Hyundai-Kia employees are connected to Monika's connections, they are listed first. Sure enough, there was man named Simon who was listed at the top of her list, and he shared a connection with me. Monika emailed me explaining her situation and asking if I could introduce her to Simon from Hyundai-Kia. I introduced the two, and they now have a meeting set up for when Monika arrives in South Korea. You never know who might be connected to the executives that you want to meet.

## SETTING UP YOUR LINKEDIN PROFILE

If you haven't already joined LinkedIn, I suggest you add that to your to-do list. It's a great tool for maintaining a professional identity, keeping track of contacts, and you will use this once you are in the work force!

## ADDING CONTACTS

When adding contacts from your address books on your various social networks and email accounts, check out what LinkedIn groups they are part of and join them. LinkedIn groups are like professional versions of Facebook groups. The majority of them are for the purpose of networking. For example, people who join the Intern Queen LinkedIn group are all interested in internship opportunities and starting conversations about internship experiences. You will be surprised what great connections you can make through these groups.

## YOUR RESUME ON LINKEDIN

Use LinkedIn to help you organize your experience. Block out an hour or so to set up your profile and be thorough. Your professional resume needs to be one page. In contrast, your LinkedIn resume can be as long as you'd like. Just remember that executives will be looking at this. Watch your spelling and use consistent formatting and punctuation.

Keep your profile updated. Executives obsess over LinkedIn and constantly change and update their profiles. Anytime you leave a job or internship, be sure to note that on your LinkedIn profile. As you add employers to your resume, search for them on LinkedIn and follow their company. You can also add executives on LinkedIn as your contacts. I suggest not trying to add them until your internship is over. Many executives (including myself) find it inappropriate to friend someone on any social network while the internship takes place.

## LINKEDIN RECOMMENDATIONS

Under your Profile section, you will find a tab that reads Recommendations. Although you need hard copy or electronic files for letters of recommendation, LinkedIn recommendations are great for your internship search and also for your job hunt. After your internship, feel free to connect with past employers and internship coordinators over LinkedIn. At the end of your internship, ask them if you can connect with them on LinkedIn and if they would mind adding a recommendation for you on LinkedIn. To do this, click on Recommendations, and the tab that says *Request Recommendations*. You can do this for character, academic, and professional references. In order to request a recommendation, you will have to send them a note through LinkedIn. Don't use the template note that shows up as a default on the site. Personalize everything you send out. Let's say that I'm in college and I'm reaching out to Autumn, my first internship coordinator at the Zimmerman Agency. Here is an example of what my note might say:

Dear Autumn,

How are you? Hope all is well. I wanted to reach out and request a recommendation from you on my LinkedIn page. I had such a great experience interning at your company and would love for future employers to learn more about what I accomplished. Thank you so much!

Best,
Lauren Berger
University of Central Florida '14

## LINKEDIN STATUS UPDATES

In comparison to Twitter and Facebook, LinkedIn is the least social and the most professional network. Keep this in mind when you update your status on the network. I don't suggest using social connector widgits to link your Twitter and LinkedIn as the status functions are read by different audiences. Don't do this unless you are comfortable with all of your professional LinkedIn contacts reading what you write on Twitter.

# USE FACEBOOK, TWITTER, AND LINKEDIN TO LAND JOBS

Now that you understand how to set up and monitor each of these networks, I want to explain how to use these networks to land internships. First, you must monitor and track your target employers on all three social networks that we've reviewed. Then, you engage and connect with the brand over the network they use the most frequently.

## Monitor Employers on Facebook, Twitter, and LinkedIn

By monitoring an employer's online presence, you keep yourself up to date on that company's clients, news, and special opportunities and you better understand a company culture.

In chapter 2, we spoke about the Intern Queen Dream List, so let's pull that document out. You identified ten employers as *target* employers on that list. Open three tabs on your computer: Facebook.com, Twitter.com, and LinkedIn.com. It's time to search for all of these employers on each one of your social networks (now that you've signed up). Each one of these networks has a search bar at the top of the user homepage where you can type in the name of the company and see if they have an official presence on the network. To be clear, you are looking for an official company page, not an individual or personal profile. On Twitter.com, it might be more helpful to click Who to Follow at the top of the screen and type your target employer into that search box. When you find a target employer on one or more social networks, note that on your Intern Queen Dream List. For Facebook, you want to *like* the company, on Twitter and LinkedIn you will *follow* the company. Remember to utilize the list functionality on Twitter and add all target employers to a private list so that you can view updates from your target employers whenever you'd like. Do you need to follow these employers on every network every day? No, but I suggest selecting a day that you are the least busy and using that as your catch-up day. Start a list called your Weekend Read and print out or bookmark each article that you want to read over the weekend. This will keep you up-to-date with everything on the employer's page.

Over time, you will find that you are drawn to specific companies' information over others'. Perhaps one company consistently tweets out links that you find useful or pointers that you find yourself remembering or reciting back. This is how you will begin to separate and rank your target employers.

## Connecting with Employers over Facebook, Twitter, and LinkedIn

Once you are frequently monitoring your target employers, you can start to engage in conversation and connect with them. Remember, one key reason brands use social media is to connect with their audience. Brands monitor what consumers say about them on Twitter. Even if you aren't directly sending them a message, type their brand name into the search bar and see what comes up. For example, my Samsung camera malfunctioned, so I tweeted, "My Samsung camera is broken. What can I do?" Within the hour, I had a direct message from a customer service representative on Twitter who monitors the use of the word *Samsung* with clear instructions on how to mail back my camera and get a replacement. I never in a million years thought that if I tweeted, "I don't like the Detroit Airport. I missed my flight" that the Detroit Airport would be tracking the tweets written about them and tweet me back to say, "What's wrong @Internqueen? How can we improve?" We live in a world where brands live and die by their customers and go above and beyond to directly connect with the consumer.

My advice is to slowly build a relationship with these employers by starting a conversation. Test the waters by liking, sharing, or retweeting their updates. By doing this, you are not only starting to engage, you are syndicating their content. By sharing or retweeting their messages or links, you've helped their brand message reach an entirely new audience—your network. When employers check their Facebook or Twitter @ replies, they will notice your mention, post, or retweet. Will they respond? Probably not, but you can be 80 percent sure they read the message and saw your name. You want to slowly have them recognize your name time after time.

Once you feel comfortable, start to actually leave comments on the employers' updates via Facebook, Twitter, or LinkedIn. If they ask questions, answer them. If they list a helpful link, write why you thought it was helpful. Once you get a hang of these networks, send the employer a direct message. Ask about internship opportunities at their company and how to apply. If you've already applied for their internship, politely let them know. Any familiarity they can associate with your name is a good thing. Just don't be pushy and bother them.

Read over employers' tweets or status updates and constantly ask yourself, "How can I add value to this conversation?" Think about questions they've tweeted that you can answer, relevant articles that may address questions or comments they've made, or send them a direct message and ask about opportunities.

Another tip is to search the executives from the company (find the names on the company website or by search engine). Check to see if any of the executives have his or her own Twitter page. If the Twitter streams look work related, go ahead—message the executive and try to connect.

To better examine how these interactions work, meet Martin. He attends UCLA and is obsessed with *Complex* magazine. He located the editor of *Complex* on Twitter and started religiously reading his tweets. He constantly retweeted (RT'd) helpful links and information from the *Complex* editor's personal Twitter page. The editor noticed his fan and was responsive when Martin reached out through a direct message (DM) and asked about internship opportunities. Currently Martin interns at *Complex* magazine, and the editor has taken particular interest in his growth at the company. I hear these stories quite frequently.

In fact, I received an email today (as I'm writing this) from another student, Julio, who interacted with me over Twitter years ago. He found me when he was researching internship experts and sent me a few messages asking specific internship questions. Today he sent me a Twitter message that said "@internqueen I have exciting news for you! Check your email." I had the following message from Julio:

Hi Lauren!

Back in February, I tweeted the Partners Trust, a boutique brokers and acquisitions office based in Los Angeles, and the CEO responded to my tweet. We have since been communicating, and I had my interview on Monday. I will be starting off as a social media intern for ten weeks; we'll see where we go from there. Next week I go back to Beverly Hills to meet with the social media team to discuss the logistics. I'm so excited! I just thought I would share with you.

Sincerely,
Julio G.[5]

LinkedIn provides the ability to search specific employees and job titles at target companies and find out who you might share connections with. If you really want to intern for Hasbro and cannot locate the internship coordinator, you could type "Hasbro human resources" into the LinkedIn search bar and see which executives come up. You will also see what connections you share with those employees. This information is extremely valuable especially when internships aren't listed as opportunities on the company website.

LinkedIn also enables users to search by alumni. University alumni centers are sometimes disorganized or not able to stay up to date. Use LinkedIn to find out where some of your school's alumni are working and what types of companies they're at. Your school major or department might also have a LinkedIn group to join, so search that as well. Getting in the door is always easier with some sort of mutual friend or contact.

# SETTING UP YOUR BLOG

Blogging can be another way for students to prove their knowledge of social media. I argue that blogging is and will continue to be an important component of any industry and is not limited to media-related fields. Commonly students blog about trends and their thoughts and perspectives on current events, college life, and interesting articles they read and have opinions about. If you don't have a dream career at this point, blog strictly about the things that do interest you. Blog about a favorite band, a favorite store, or anything you've experienced. Share your world and your thoughts with readers. At the beginning of this chapter, I mentioned my Florida State University ambassador, Chandra. Her blog is all about fashion as she dreams of working in the fashion industry. She blogs about deals she finds on must-have items, trends she thinks other women her age should note, internship advice, and noteworthy experiences. Chandra's blog helped her land two internships. She showed her potential employers her blog, and they said it showed initiative, self-motivation, and her strong writing skills. Chandra even says that she's been recognized on campus because her blog is read by so many of her classmates.

Follow Chandra's lead and start blogging. I suggest using Wordpress, as it's a free, easy-to-use platform for blogging (www.wordpress.com). But a blog is a commitment. A blog with two entries is not impressive. You don't need to blog every day, but you do need to blog consistently, so decide how many times per week you will blog and put together a blogging schedule for yourself. I'd rather see a student with no blog than a student with a blog who updated it six months ago. Show employers that when you start projects and commit to something, you follow through.

When you first launch your blog, try to add a few entries. I wouldn't start promoting your blog until you have five pieces of content. When a user comes to your blog, you want to keep that user there with plenty of fresh content.

# What Should My Blog Include?

When I talk about blogs that stand out to employers, I mean blogs that present a specific perspective on a subject, show your voice, highlight your personality, and showcase trends you've explored. I'm not talking about blogs that express negative thoughts or opinions. Expressing negative opinions on controversial topics translates poorly to an employer. Proceed at your own risk. If your blog is relevant to the position you are applying for, include it on your resume. However, if the blog showcases any sort of negative or provocative language, I would not include this on a resume, as this can hinder you from getting the position.

# Getting Your Blog Out to the World

Syndicating content is key, and the best tools for that are Facebook, Twitter, and LinkedIn. You already have an organic following off Facebook. The people who are your Facebook friends follow your status updates and are already tied to you in some way. Use Facebook as a means to share and syndicate new content. The idea is that they will click once and then become regular subscribers through your blog's RSS feed, which delivers automatic, timely updates. Twitter and LinkedIn help generate retweets, comments, and start conversations.

Also, don't be afraid to tell people about your blog. At internqueen.com, word of mouth is still our most powerful form of traffic. Your energy (like mine) can be contagious. Tell your friends you've started blogging and you are really excited about it. Eventually you could have your friends contribute to your blog. This gets them excited about the blog and gives you their organic network as they will most likely share their own content with their online communities and friends.

- Set up profiles on Facebook, Twitter, and LinkedIn, if you haven't already.
- Take a moment to think about your personal brand and the image you'd like to project to future employers.
- Block out two hours on a weekend to go through all of the photos you currently have uploaded to Facebook and the pictures you are tagged in. Remove any tags and photos that are questionable. Remember, if you untag yourself in something, no one can retag you.
- Set aside time to approach friends who may be posting inappropriate pictures on Facebook.
- Review your Facebook profile and wall to make sure they are employer proof. Enable your privacy settings and the function that emails you every time you are tagged in a new photo.
- Decide what your social media hours are. At what point in your day can you go online for a predetermined amount of time to check your messages and look at friends' or employers' updates?
- Download the Facebook and Twitter applications to your phone so you use them on the go instead of while you should be working or studying.
- Set aside time to create your Twitter lists to organize who you follow.
- On LinkedIn, make sure your resume is up-to-date and you are connected with your past employers.
- Request at least three recommendations on LinkedIn from previous employers.
- Take out your Intern Queen Dream List and look up each employer on Facebook, Twitter, and LinkedIn.
- Start monitoring your employer's profiles on each network. Pick a catch-up day each week to check out any interesting articles they may have added to their status updates.

- As appropriate, start to comment or send messages to employers.
- Determine if you'd like to start blogging. Set up a free blog at Wordpress or your favorite blogging platform and get to work!

You've made it. Social media is quite powerful, and I hope that after reading through this entire chapter, you realize that. You now understand how to develop and leverage your personal brand in order to help you land amazing internship opportunities. So many students use Facebook, Twitter, and LinkedIn socially but forget to use it professionally—you will be able to do both. With your new profiles, appropriate content, and time management techniques, social media will slowly become a good friend and a great tool in the internship process. I guarantee that employers will take notice of your online efforts. Remember to become a good listener and think about the message employers are trying to project about their companies. This is going to help you figure out where you want to work and which company is the right fit for you. Once you become a good listener, you have free rein to reach out and connect with these employers. Good luck, I'll be here for you throughout the entire experience.

Now that your applications are out and your social media profiles are perfected, we can move on to the interview process. I will explain the new types of interviews, touch on the traditional interviews, and give you tons of advice from dress code to practice questions. Let's continue, shall we?

## CHAPTER 5

# Rock the
# **Interview**

Up to this point, every personal story I've shared has been about my experience as an intern. We all know that internships lead to job opportunities, at that specific company or at another. I want to share an experience I had after college that illustrates both the power of internship contacts and the power of a solid interview. After college, I moved to Los Angeles to pursue a career in the entertainment industry. My internship contacts always told me the best way to start in Hollywood was to work at a talent agency. I called a contact of mine at FOX, who I had met on internship the previous summer, and asked if he knew how I should start my career path. He asked if I researched where I wanted to work. I told him that everyone I spoke with encouraged me to seek out assistant positions at talent agencies. Everyone would say, "It's the best place to learn the business from the inside out." My contact at FOX asked if there was a specific talent agency I wanted to work at. "CAA; they are the best," I enthusiastically replied.

Within twenty-four hours of that conversation, I received a phone call from the head of human resources at Creative Artists Agency (CAA). Little did I know, that phone call would change my life forever.

I interviewed with a young talent agent with a *nice guy* reputation, fairly uncommon for the talent agent world. Looking back on the interview, I was unprepared. I barely knew anything about an assistant's role at an agency. The agent drilled me on whether or not I was ready for such a tough position. He spoke fast and warned me, "This job requires 100 percent of your focus all of the time, working long hours, lots of overtime, being a pure perfectionist, having great relationship-building skills, and so much more." I faked a smile through my nerves, but I'm sure I looked overwhelmed. I didn't get the position and was told that the agent didn't think I was ready. I was crushed.

Two days later, I was in the Nordstrom dressing room when my phone rang. Miraculously it was CAA, and they wanted me to come in later that day for an interview with another talent agent named Tracy. I vowed not to repeat my earlier mistakes as I now understood the importance of preparing for an interview. I researched Tracy and was pleased to find she was quite the powerhouse Hollywood agent with big names on her repertoire like Demi Moore, Aaron Eckhart, and Nicolas Cage. I phoned a few friends and contacts from other internships and asked what they knew about her. Everyone sort of laughed and said, "Oh, Tracy—good luck!" I didn't know if I should be excited or scared.

I planned my interview attire carefully, selecting a black business suit, black pointed-toe heels, and a bold colorful necklace to show I had some personality. I purchased an oversized black work bag that looked polished and could hold everything from my portfolio to my makeup.

When I think back, that day feels like a dream sequence. I remember pushing open the heavy doors to the old CAA building off Little Santa Monica Road in Beverly Hills. I think the 90210 theme song was on repeat in my brain! I checked in with the front desk, "Hello, I'm Lauren Berger and here for an interview with Tracy."

I remember waiting—and then realizing that I'd been waiting for over forty-five minutes. I looked around to see if anyone noticed how long I'd been sitting in the atrium. No one seemed surprised or like it was anything other than normal. Finally I was greeted by a skinny assistant with glasses, Mark. He was apologetic but told me that Tracy running late was very normal. I can still feel all of the other assistants' eyes on me as I was guided through the halls of the talent agency. Mark escorted me into Tracy's office and said, "Tracy, this is Lauren. Enjoy." And he was gone. It was just the two of us.

A gorgeous tall brunette turned around. Her office was everything I'd want my office to look like—turquoise sofa, brown comfy pillows, cute picture frames everywhere with portraits of her family and celebrity clients. Tracy was dressed in all black, spike heels, and tons of jewelry—quite the power woman.

She starting apologizing for running late but kept saying, "That's how it goes around here." I smiled and pretended I knew what she meant. I had no clue. During the interview, I made sure to speak clearly and explain how my previous internship experience helped shape my skill set and experience level. She was very curious about why I wanted to interview for CAA and I replied with the honest answer, "I've had several internships in the entertainment business over the years at Fox, MTV, NBC, and others, and everyone I've spoken with tells me the best way to start in this industry is at a talent agency like CAA." Tracy proceeded to try and scare me away, warning me of the long hours, the cut-throat environment, and the multiple tasks I would be expected to conduct at once. I looked her in the eye and told her that I was passionate and 100 percent certain about this position. I remember her last question vividly, "If I offered you the job today, would you need some time to think it over?"

"Nope. This is what I want to do, and I'm ready to start tomorrow," I replied.

My performance won me the job, and I became the second assistant to Tracy, head of motion picture talent at CAA, for two years. They were the most educational two years of my life, both personally and professionally. My life would be completely different today if I hadn't rocked that interview and hadn't had the initial internship at FOX that connected me to the opportunity at CAA.

As a prospective intern, you'll also need to master entry-level interviewing skills. You may feel overwhelmed or nervous at first, but with practice and by following the tips in this chapter, you'll soon be an interview pro. The goal of this chapter is to help you develop a strong understanding of each type of interview—over the phone, in person, via Skype, and the "Starbucks interview." I offer different tips and tricks for mastering each interview type. Additionally, I'll walk you through the interview process from the first professional correspondence with the employer through the follow-up email and thank-you note that you write after the interview. It's imperative to respond to an employer's email request in the right way, and I'll provide templates and examples for various situations that might arise. I'll also cover what to wear, what questions to prepare for, and how to make a lasting impression. The interview is the *almost there* point—it's the last hurdle to jump before landing the position. If you make it through the interview and impress the employer, you are golden. If you mess up the interview, your chances of getting hired are slim. By the end of this chapter, you will be confident in your ability to give a great interview.

# UNDERSTANDING THE FOUR TYPES OF INTERVIEWS

The two most common interviews are the phone interview and the in-person interview. In today's fast-paced society, employers want interns and they want them quickly, so the phone interview is increasingly popular. If employers conduct multiple rounds of interviews, they begin with a phone interview and conduct an in-person interview to follow. However, I'm here to introduce and confirm the existence of two other interviews—the Skype interview and what I've termed the "Starbucks interview." Below I explain each of the four most common interviews and give detailed pointers for each one.

## Interview Type #1: The Phone Interview

Phone interviews help employers decide if students can represent the employer well. Can they carry a conversation? Do they speak clearly, professionally, and with confidence? Do they know how to get to the point or do they tend to ramble? The phone interview is the most common type of interview. And it makes sense—they are easy to do and require little effort on the employer's part. During a phone interview, you must keep the employer's full attention focused on your conversation. Many employers get easily distracted with work in front of them—they may be looking at emails, typing correspondence, browsing on the Internet, or any number of other tasks.

Hold the attention of the employer by constantly tying answers back to that company and what it does. This concept is similar to what we discussed in chapter 2 regarding cover letters. On the phone interview, pay close attention to the volume at which you speak. You must speak up, speak clearly and slowly. If the employer cannot understand what you say in the first two sentences, you have officially lost that employer for the rest of the call. For some reason, many students pointlessly ramble on phone interviews. It might be nerves, or perhaps the desire to impress the employer. Make sure that your answers are focused.

When doing a phone interview, be aware of your surroundings. Do your best to be in an environment you can control. Test the phone first. Make sure you have reception. Try to do the call from home or school. If you are driving (in a state where it's legal to drive while on the phone) or using a Bluetooth during the interview, you could hit a spot with bad reception and drop the call. I suggest pulling over where you do have service to make the call. If you have a GPS on while driving, turn it off when you do your interview so it doesn't talk and interrupt you! If you are doing the call from your apartment or dorm room, make sure to tell your roommates what you are doing (the same will go for Skype interviews). You don't want them walking in and asking "What's up?" during the actual phone interview. Make sure that any dogs barking, toilets flushing, roommates yelling, doors slamming, and other general disturbances are kept down to a minimum during this process. (I'm serious, this stuff happens.)

## Interview Type #2: The In-Person Interview

Since completing fifteen internships, I've had my fair share of at least fifty in-person interviews. Now that I run my own business, I've been on the other side of the desk and interviewed several individuals for jobs and internships with my company. I've also done consulting for companies that need help interviewing students, including helping them to ask the right types of questions.

When I interviewed in Orlando at the *Daily Buzz*, a nationally syndicated morning show, they lined up chairs in the television studio and used a group interview format. They asked us questions about our previous experience. We went around in a circle answering the questions, each potential candidate trying to up-stage the person sitting next to them. Although this group interview format was intimidating, I used my energy and knowledge of the television show to stand out from the rest. Before I went into the interview, I recorded a week's worth of episodes so I was very familiar with the show.

BWR Public Relations in Los Angeles refused to hire me as an intern before conducting an in-person interview. I couldn't afford to fly out to Los Angeles before the summer, so I accepted another part-time unpaid internship and crossed my fingers. When I arrived in Los Angeles at the beginning of the summer, I interviewed with the company. The interviewer and I sat at a never-ending conference table. What was I asked? "Are you 100 percent sure you want the position?" I said yes. I landed the internship (and scheduled it for the days I wasn't working at the other internship). Phew!

Normally the in-person interview consists of the student and the internship coordinator or human resources executive sitting together in an office or conference room. This is good ole face-to-face communication.

At an in-person interview, you shake hands with the employer. Your handshake should be firm and last for only a few seconds. Don't grab too lightly, too hard, or hold on too long. Practice a firm handshake with your friends and family. Keep your wrist straight. When you meet an employer, make eye contact and smile. Always introduce yourself by your first and last name. When you first meet someone, be formal, as you want people to think of you as a professional, not a child. Make sure that you walk straight with your head held high and not slumped over. Appear confident—it goes a long way. After we discuss the final two types of interviews, we will dive into interview preparation and how to make a lasting impression.

# Interview Type #3: Skype Interviews

A year ago I traveled to Dayton, Ohio, to speak at Central State University. The career fair landed on the same day as my visit, so I observed the event and chatted with students and local employers. I watched as a young man introduced himself very professionally to one of the featured employers. He passed along his resume and got the employer's business card. The employer looked over the student's resume on the spot and told the student he wanted to schedule an interview.

The student was pleased, "Yes! Absolutely. When would you like me to come in for an interview?"

"Actually we don't do in-person interviews anymore. Only Skype," announced the employer.

*What?* An alarm went off in my head. Skype interviews were happening, and I wasn't sure anyone really knew or believed it.

"Umm . . . I've never done a Skype interview before and I don't have a webcam," the student responded.

The employer paused and looked at the student and said, "All right then, we'll be in touch if we have something for you."

You cannot hesitate. Your hesitation causes the employer to question your interest in the position. You must prepare for Skype interviews as they pop up regularly within many different industries. In fact, some employers prefer Skype to phone interviews. Skype interviews allow employers to learn more about the candidate as they are able to see how the student presents themselves. In a Skype interview, dress as you would for an in-person interview. Students ask me all of the time if they need to wear pants to a Skype interview. The answer is yes! Again, I'll provide a style guide for interviews in the dress code section later in this chapter.

Andrea, my campus ambassador from Ohio University, interviewed at a professional styling company in New York City. Her first round of interviews was over the phone. The second round was over Skype with the CEO of the company. She dressed just as she would for an in-person interview over Skype. She didn't have a webcam so it was her responsibility to figure out where she could find one. Andrea is a great example of a student who was making things happen even when it wasn't the most convenient. Although she ended up accepting another opportunity, the experience proved to her how vital it is to understand the Skype interview process.

Most career service centers have webcams in the office for students to use for both mock and real Skype interviews. The key with Skype interviews is to be prepared. Ask your career center staff if they have webcam. If not, check with your local library, friends, or family. Most new laptops come with built in webcams. The key is to be prepared and know where you can do a Skype interview if the opportunity presents itself.

With both Skype and phone interviews, you must regulate outside noise and interruptions—but in addition, with Skype you must also be aware of what's around you (visually speaking). If your dorm room has inappropriate pictures or posters in the background or looks messy, you don't want to do a Skype interview from that location. Make sure that you put time into creating a professional background—even if it's just a white wall. You can test your video settings on Skype under Call and Video Options just to make sure you look presentable and the background looks professional. I suggest doing a practice Skype video call with a friend to make sure everything looks in place. When speaking with someone over Skype, be sure to look into the camera on your computer and avoid starring at the image of yourself. People can tell where your eyes are focused. Think of your webcam as the person's eyes—it's the Skype version of eye contact. If any interruption should happen and your call gets fuzzy or you lose an Internet signal, ask the employer if you can call right back. You could say, "I'm so sorry, my Skype seems to be freezing up. May I call you back in one minute? I want to make sure I hear everything clearly."

If you've never used Skype before, here are some tips on setting up your profile:

- Go to Skype.com and click Get Skype and then Download Now. You can use Skype for instant messaging, audio calls, audio conferencing, video calls, and now video conferencing. If you purchase an external webcam, you can use that for your video. You can purchase an inexpensive webcam for under ten dollars from a variety of retailers.

- Follow the prompts to create your Skype user profile. Make sure your username is professional. I suggest using your first and last name and keeping it simple. Use this for professional purposes and to communicate with friends.
- Skype runs an automatic test on your computer to ensure everything works properly. Just like other social networks, it allows you to import your contacts from other email accounts that already have Skype.

## Interview Type #4: The Starbucks Interview

When I first wrote the outline for this book, I didn't include the Starbucks interview. As time has passed, I've received more and more questions from students who have upcoming coffee shop interviews. The Starbucks interview is not exclusive to Starbucks; it can be at any coffee shop, restaurant, or other public meeting place. Executives who work from home virtually or just want to take a break from the office conduct these interviews. I work from a coffee shop a majority of the day, and I've overheard several of these interviews. Recently a casting director was interviewing an intern at a local Coffee Bean and after greeting one another, the employer said, "So let's get down to business: why you?" That's a no-nonsense first question and a tough question. You must have an answer ready to explain why you are the best person for the position. In a public place, this question can seem even more overwhelming. You look around and see others in the coffee shop watching you and might feel embarrassed. Take a deep breath and remember, this is your time, your interview, and you owe it to yourself to give the best possible interview—even if it may seem like the entire coffee shop is listening and eagerly awaiting your responses.

In the style section below, I'll address the proper attire for a coffee shop interview. The biggest thing to remember is to take the interview seriously and conduct yourself professionally. Yes, this interview is out of the office, but that doesn't mean you should be any less amazing. When you walk into that coffee shop, you should turn heads. Everyone should already know that you are going to kill it and land the internship or job.

We know there are hundreds of Starbucks, Coffee Bean, and Dunkin Donuts locations across the country. Make sure that you confirm the location where the interview is and get the exact address and cross streets so you don't end up at the coffee shop around the corner from your employer.

I like to show up early for the interview, purchase my own coffee, and select the least awkward place for us to sit. Normally this means a table in the corner, away from the main line and the crowds.

# RESPONDING TO AN INTERVIEW REQUEST

Now that you understand the four most common interview scenarios, let's address how you should respond to an employer's initial interview request via phone or email. If I'm an employer, I receive a student's resume and cover letter and review them at my convenience. If I believe the student has potential, I'll either call or email to request an interview. In my mind, the student has approximately twenty-four hours to get back to me and convince me the internship is a priority for him or her.

There are a few different scenarios that may occur after you receive this email or phone request. I've included guidelines and templates on the following pages to assist you in handling interview requests. I've addressed each note to Ashley Art, the fictional internship coordinator for WWWW Radio Station, a fictional station.

## You've Already Accepted Another Position

If you've already accepted another internship that you are completely happy with, kindly email or call the employer back and say that you've already accepted another position and thank the employer for the opportunity. If the employer called you, call the employer back. If the employer emailed you, respond with an email. Here is a sample email that you would send to an employer in this situation.

Dear Ashley Art,

Thank you so much for responding to my internship application and requesting an interview. I feel honored to be considered for the position. Unfortunately I have to decline the interview as I've already accepted another position. I know your time is valuable. Thank you so much for your time and I hope that our paths cross again in the future.

Best,
Lauren Berger
University of Central Florida '14
Phone: 555-555-5555, Email: lberger@gmail.com

## You Aren't Interested in the Internship

You were eager to apply and didn't read through all of the necessary information. Oops.

This situation happens frequently. Always respond to the employer. I can't stress how frequently people change jobs and how small the world is. Do not ignore employer's emails. Doing so will come back to bite you. There is nothing worse than being unresponsive when an employer has gone out of his or her way to get in touch with you. The employer only has your information because *you* passed it along. Write or call the employer back. Executives and professionals are very sensitive about their time and want to make sure their time isn't wasted. You must acknowledge this in your response. This is what you should email or say:

Dear Ashley Art,

Thank you so much for getting back to me about my internship application. Unfortunately I've decided to pursue other opportunities that I feel will better suit my career path. I do realize your time is valuable and thank you again for considering my application. I hope we can stay in touch.

Best,
Lauren Berger
University of Central Florida '14
Phone: 555-555-5555, Email: lberger@gmail.com

# You Are Interested, But . . .

Perhaps you'll be out of town or unavailable at the times they've suggested. Always do whatever is in your power to make yourself available. The only exceptions are if you know you will be in an area with no phone reception or you have class, work, or an internship. If you cannot make the times the employer suggests, explain your reason briefly, and suggest three other times that work for you. If you only suggest one other time that you are available, employers might interpret this as you feeling entitled. Employers shouldn't move their entire day around to accommodate an intern's schedule. You always cater to the employer as best you can. Noah Dinkin, president of FanBridge, a successful start-up that manages fan bases for influencers like musicians and athletes, scheduled an interview with a student for a Thursday at 9 a.m. The student failed to tell Noah that he would be driving across the country with his family at that time. Noah tried connecting with the student on Thursday at 9 a.m., and they played phone tag for about two hours because the student had limited cell phone reception. The student should have explained to Noah that he planned to drive across the country and suggested some times that he knew he could speak. Noah found it too hard to connect with this student, and after three rounds of phone tag, he called it quits. He hired another intern. Don't make hiring you an impossible task.

## You Are Available

Get excited! You never know where an interview can take you. Try to respond within twenty-four hours. This is what your call or email should say:

Dear Ashley Art,

Thank you so much for your email. I would love to schedule an interview as I'm extremely interested in the internship position. I have classes in the mornings and can be available any day after 11 a.m. EST. I look forward to speaking with you.

Best,
Lauren Berger
University of Central Florida '14
Phone: 555-555-5555, Email: lberger@gmail.com

From the previous examples, I hope you understand the on-going theme of always being responsive to an employer and never avoiding an email or call. Every business is based on relationships, and burning bridges is something that no student or professional can afford to do.

# PREPARATION FOR INTERVIEWS

Many of you probably had an imaginary friend when you were younger. Let's make up an imaginary intern. We'll call her Dana, the ideal intern. Dana is a junior at Purdue and applying to intern at the Indiana Chamber of Commerce during her summer semester. She knows that preparation is key, so before the interview, she visits the company website, makes a list of her learning objectives for the internship, visits her career center, reviews practice questions, and makes a list of her own questions to ask the employer at the end of the interview. The entire preparation process takes Dana one day on campus visiting the career center and a few hours of prep on her own in her dorm. Dana is overly prepared for her interview. Her chances of landing the position just went from zero to sixty. Can you be an ideal interview candidate? Can you do what Dana did? Of course! Just keep reading as I break down each part of the preparation process and explain exactly how you can accomplish what Dana was able to.

## Step 1: Research the Company Website

You started the research process when you filled out the Intern Queen Dream List and wrote your cover letter. More than likely, it's been a few weeks since you researched the company, so it's time to work a bit more. Go right to the company website. Examine the company mission statement, which is normally found under the *About Us* section. You studied this section while writing the cover letter; now you want to remember the company language and buzz words to incorporate in the interview. When I say this, I don't mean that you should recite the company mission statement to the employer, but you should reference it. For example, if the employer asks what drew you to the company, you could say something like, "I looked over the company website and mission statement, and I feel strongly about the cause and really believe in the goals of the organization."

By the end of the interview, the employer *should* know that you were on the company website; it shouldn't be a question. You want the employer to know that you took the time to research the company.

While on the company website, check out any recent news, updated client lists, or portfolios, and get a strong sense of the founders and executive team. You need to know what the company does. When the employer says, "Do you understand what we do?" Your response should be, "Yes, I've reviewed the company website and read up on the organization. I'd love to hear more about it and of course about the internship program." Make sure you don't only understand what they do but can actually articulate it to someone. Practice by telling a friend or family member what the company does. Oftentimes we understand a concept or idea but have difficulty putting it into words. If you need to just talk to yourself and practice saying it out loud, go ahead.

Researching ahead of time puts you on the same page as the employer. Communication comes more naturally when you are on the same page. Popular interview questions that preinterview research can help with are these:

- What sort of clients do we have that excite you?
- Who do you see yourself working with at our company?
- Why do you want to work at our company?


Keep a notebook with you during the research process and take notes on everything you find and think will be useful if brought up during the interview. Review your notes the night before the interview and right before the interview.

# Step 2: Make Your List of Learning Objectives

In the chapters to follow, we're going to explore techniques to make the most of your internship. Students walk into internships very excited about the opportunity, but they forget to take advantage of it. Making a list of learning objectives before the internship not only helps you at the interview, but it will also help you at the beginning, middle, and end of your internship. When I say *learning objectives*, I mean a list of the goals you know you want to achieve or the things you know you want to learn. My first internship was at the Zimmerman Agency, a public relations and advertising firm. Before I started the position, my learning objectives for the company were as follows:

- Learn about the public relations industry
- Observe how to manage professional relationships
- Watch how account managers deal with their clients and the media
- Write a press release or help write a press release

You can tell by this list that I didn't know much about the specific intern duties at the Zimmerman Agency, but what I did know, I found online during the research phase. When I started my internship, I learned more about the company and the internship program and was able to tweak my list. The goal of having this list of learning objectives is to answer an employer's question when you're asked, "What do you want to get out of this opportunity?" By defining and focusing on your goals and desires, you'll end up getting more out of the interview process.

# Step 3: Visit the Career Center

The career center is the most overlooked and underutilized part of the internship equation. You've heard me say it before, and I'm saying it again—go into the career center. During your internship preparation phase, you want to visit the career center for two purposes: mock interviews and practice questions.

Mock interviews are scheduled by appointment with a career counselor, normally through the career center website or by walking into the center and scheduling with the front desk. Dress the part and have a rehearsal interview. The career center representative evaluates your performance and provides helpful feedback on your interview skills and style. Let's say you go into an interview and you bomb it, but you don't know why. Well, you just lost a position that could have potentially been saved had you gone into the career center and done the mock interview. Perhaps you were twirling your hair too much or speaking too softly or your answers weren't up to par. These are criticisms that the career center provides for free, so you don't miss out on an opportunity.

The second reason to walk into the career center is to get a list of practice questions for your interview. Take a copy or make a copy of your own and review these practice questions.

## Practice the Practice Questions!

Now let's go over some of the most frequently asked questions for internship interviews. Remember, just reading over the list of questions won't do you much good. You must be prepared to answer each question succinctly and intelligently. Show them what a great intern you'd be and why!

### WHY YOU?

The interviewer is basically asking, "Why are you the best candidate for the position?" This question puts you on the spot and may throw you off. You don't want to sound desperate, but you also don't want to sound overly confident. How do you answer?

Point to the facts. What skills and experience do you have that make you qualified for this experience? If you don't have previous internship experience, what relevant training have you done? Are you in a club at school? Do you hold a position in a sorority or fraternity? Have you taken relevant coursework? Think outside of the box.

## CAN YOU TELL ME A LITTLE ABOUT YOURSELF?

Career coaches say employers ask you to "tell me about yourself," to see if you are a good fit for the position. I disagree. Employers ask you this question when they haven't prepared for the interview *or* to see how you carry a conversation. They want to get an initial sense of your communication skills. If they cannot understand you, the interview is over.

You must make sure you do not trail off or go into specific detail about your experiences because you risk losing the employer's attention. Your answer includes where you went to school, your major, and why you want to work at that company. Keep answers short, sweet, and to the point. If the employer wants to know more, he or she will ask follow-up questions.

Just like when you wrote your cover letter, you must bring your answers back to the company. Constantly ask yourself how your experience and accomplishments are beneficial to that company. And then tell the employer exactly how you (and your experience) can help the company!

## WHAT IS YOUR BIGGEST WEAKNESS?

This question can have a dual meaning. Some employers ask this because it's a traditional interview question and they want to see how prepared you are. They listen to your answer and want to hear how you handle a question like this under pressure. Another reason employers might be asking this is to gauge your honesty and self-awareness. Be careful answering this question as you don't want to put your foot in your mouth. Avoid being too detailed in your response. A great way to answer this question is by telling the employer a lesson you learned at a previous internship or job. Here's an example: "At my last internship, I learned to pay more attention to detail. I didn't realize when scheduling a meeting, it was so important to ask questions, take notes, and think ahead. Paying attention to detail is a weakness of mine, but because I've recognized it and I'm actively working to improve it, I think it will become a strength."

## WHY ARE YOU INTERESTED IN THIS COMPANY?

This is where your preinterview research comes into play. When asked this question, mention that you've been on the company website, you are familiar with the founders and the clients, and you are interested in the position because of A, B, and C reasons. You should have three solid reasons why this position appeals to you.

## WHAT RELEVANT EXPERIENCE DO YOU HAVE?

When asked this question, try not to simply list off the experience you've had. Give examples. Talk about a company you worked for and a really cool project you completed during your time there. For example, my summer interns helped me execute my ideas for Intern Queen Phone, a call-in service where students can directly connect with internship coordinators who work for their dream employers. The interns identified which internship coordinators should be on the call, reached out to them, put together the promotional materials, surveyed our demographic regarding price points, and helped produce each phone call. In doing this, they learned how to professionally communicate with high-level executives, the importance of directly connecting with the demographic, and the promotion and marketing strategies that go into making a campaign work. This is precisely the type of example a student should give an employer during an interview.

But what if you don't have that level of experience? Let's look at an additional example. Samantha is interviewing for an internship with the Florida Nurses Association. They ask her about relevant experience, but she has no previous internships and really hasn't had any part-time jobs. The best experience for Samantha to draw from would be her relevant coursework, since she is a nursing major. She could also speak about class projects and how they taught her a sense of responsibility and teamwork and required a tremendous amount of focus. Samantha might also bring up how her family volunteers every year at the hospital, working with the staff to ensure the patients are comfortable and have what they need. By tying another type of relevant experience into the opportunity at hand, Samantha is still able to prove she is a great fit.

## WHAT ARE YOU HOPING TO GET OUT OF THIS INTERNSHIP?

This question asks if you have prepared for the interview and if you are serious about the process. Have you put any thought into this company? Are you applying on a whim? In answering this question, go back to the learning objectives that you created for the internship in step 2 above. This is another great time in the interview to speak about the research you've done before coming to the interview. Tell the employer that you thought about your personal learning objectives and then share those objectives. Make sure the employer knows that you plan to make your list more specific once you actually see how the company operates on a day-to-day basis and you get a sense of the opportunities available to you. This shows the employer you are taking the internship search process seriously and can really bring value, a strong work ethic, and dedication to the company team.

## WHAT ARE YOUR LONG-TERM CAREER GOALS?

This can be a tricky question to answer, especially for students who aren't clear on what they want to do. An employer hiring interns wants to select students who they can help in the long run. In other words, if the student's career goals are not in line with the company, the student might not get selected for the internship. If you are going after a high profile fashion internship and you tell the employer you want to join the Peace Corps, the employer will likely look at that as a bad fit. Hopefully all of the internships on your Intern Queen Dream List are places where you visualize yourself working in the future. Tell the employer that you feel this position benefits your career path, and emphasize your desire for a career in that industry. Avoid naming specific companies when answering this question. You never know how an employer feels about another company. And you don't want to overly praise the employer's direct competition and thereby alienate your interviewer. Remember, employers want to hear about your enthusiasm for the position they're offering above all else.

Again, a major part of an internship is that it's a learning experience that will benefit you. If you are considering an internship at a company that has nothing to do with your future plans, it's a waste of both your time and the employer's time.

## CAN YOU RECALL A SITUATION WHEN YOU WERE A LEADER AND REALLY STEPPED UP TO THE PLATE?

Be sure you're prepared to answer this type of question. Think about all of your previous experiences at internships, part-time jobs, and even inside the classroom. When were you in a crisis or problematic situation where you provided the solution? Before the interview, think of an experience you've had at work, an internship, or at school and make sure you can articulate the story well. No stories should drag on. They need to be short, sweet, and to the point.

## Preparing Questions for the Employer

Students should have one or two questions for the employer at the end of the interview to show a strong interest in the company. Keep these questions to a minimum as the employer's time is valuable. At the end of the interview, the employer likely will say, "Do you have any questions for me?" However, if the employer doesn't offer this prompt and starts to wrap up, you can interject and say, "Thank you so much for sitting down with me. Do you mind if I ask you a question that I was curious about?" When asking questions, make sure they are things the employer hasn't already answered. You don't want to give the impression that you were not listening. If the employer really does answer all of your questions, simply state, "You've actually answered all of my questions during the interview. Thank you so much." Here are a few sample questions for after the interview.

## CAN YOU DESCRIBE A TYPICAL DAY AS AN INTERN AT YOUR COMPANY?

This is my favorite question to ask because it helps you determine if the employer has your best interest as an intern at heart. The employer should know what the interns do on a daily basis. If the employer doesn't know or responds with ambiguous answers, it can be an indication that the interns have too much down time and not enough thought was put behind the program. In chapter 6, "Let's Get Legal," I'll discuss the responsibilities of the employer regarding internships.

## DO YOU HAVE ADVICE ON HOW TO MAKE THE MOST OF THIS INTERNSHIP?

Asking this question further demonstrates your commitment to the opportunity and shows that you want to step up to the plate and perform at your best. Remember what the employer says as this can be very valuable advice.

## WHAT IS THE TIME COMMITMENT REQUIRED FOR THE POSITION?

Managing expectations is important for both intern and employer. The company needs to be up front with you about the time requirements so that you can be sure this fits with your school or work schedule.

# MAKING A LASTING IMPRESSION

Ultimately you must make a lasting impression on employers so they remember you no matter how many other candidates they interview. But your answers to questions are only one component to creating a lasting impression during an interview. In this section, I will cover proper interview attire, grooming advice, tips on what to bring to the interview, and other essential interview advice.

## Interview Dress Code

Remember when you were in elementary school and you always picked out your clothes the night before? We must revert back to those days! Don't wait to figure out what to wear the day of the interview; it is a recipe for disaster. We all know that feeling of trying to get ready for an interview, date, or night out when you cannot find that one item you need. It stresses you out, changes your mood, and you end up leaving the house not feeling your best. This interview could change your life, so you must prepare. My advice is to always dress to impress and look the part. I've created a simple style guide below with two interview options each for men and women—one formal option and one almost-formal option, or what I call the "alternate interview outfit." For more interview dress information, please visit www.internqueen.com.

# Lauren's Simple Style Guide for Interviews

This is an internship book, not a style book. I could go on for days about great fashion in the workplace, but we're going to keep this simple. Before you go out and spend money on interview clothes, look through your closet and see what you already have that fits the descriptions. Again, these are the basics. If you don't own the item, you could borrow from a friend. If you can, invest in these items as they are timeless pieces and can be worn to interviews from this day forward. Remember, you don't need to spend lots of money on an item for it to work. Check out stores like H&M, Kohl's, JCPenney, Macy's, T.J. Maxx, Marshalls, and Forever 21 for the items mentioned below.

## THE FORMAL INTERVIEW OUTFIT: FOR MEN AND WOMEN

The formal interview outfit includes three pieces: the classic business suit, the best button-down shirt, and a perfect pair of shoes. (I'll also talk about accessorizing a bit later in this section.) You will notice I refer to these clothes as "pieces." I do this not only because I think it sounds more professional and polished but also because you can mix and match each item to create more than one outfit. Again, this process is about taking yourself seriously. When skimming your closet to see which pieces you might already have, please stay away from pant and jacket sets that don't match, are pilling, or just look aged. If you don't look put-together, you might not get the job. I suggest budgeting about two hundred dollars for interview clothing. If you don't want to save for this expense, rethink your priorities. And again, if you buy the right items, they can last forever. If you are super savvy, you might be able to pick up everything for even less.

If your parents have said they will help you pay for these items, be as organized as possible when you approach them about the items you'd like to buy. Have a list of exactly what your needs are.

## THE CLASSIC BUSINESS SUIT: FOR MEN AND WOMEN

There are some outfits that anyone can put on and look fabulous in—the business suit is one of them. Allow yourself to get friendly with a basic black or dark charcoal business suit. Get one that fits, get it tailored if you need, and you can wear it forever (assuming your weight doesn't fluctuate too much). The business suit is the safe bet for both men and women during the interview process.

**Women:** I'm frequently asked if a business suit needs to consist of pants or a skirt. Personally I prefer pants. I feel more comfortable in them, don't need to worry about the length like I do with a skirt, stay warm in cold offices, and don't need to worry about how I'm sitting. That being said, it's a personal preference, and a skirt and jacket combination works as well. The business suit is a great canvas for you to wear. Because it's so simple, you can dress it up or down depending on the company and position. Avoid spending money on suits with bold colors or elaborate patterns as you want something timeless.

**Men:** Stick with a dark-colored business suit: grays, charcoals, blacks. Stay away from lighter colors or trendy colors.

## THE BEST BUTTON-DOWN

Men and women benefit from investing in the perfect button-down shirt. Since white button-downs get ruined easily, you might try a pale blue or green to add some color. Feeling bold? Wear a bold red or yellow underneath your suit. If you go with white, make sure it's not completely see-through and test which undergarment you want to wear to make sure it doesn't show. You should be able to find a timeless button-down for under $60.00. Try not to buy something uber-cheap that's going to rip or deteriorate the following week. Pay close attention to the cleaning instructions. Make sure you don't shrink it, and if it needs to be dry-cleaned, take it to be dry-cleaned! Keep it nice so it lasts.

**Women:** Proceed with caution if you have a full bust. Make sure the button down covers you and fits nicely. You don't want to be concerned about a button popping open during the interview.

**Men:** Make sure that you wear the proper undershirt if you go with the button-down. Don't wear a see-through A-line tank top (aka wife beater) underneath—it's simply tacky.

## THE PERFECT PAIR OF SHOES

The shoes to buy depend on the color of your suit. If you went for the black or grey suit, black shoes are going to be your best bet. If your suit is blue or tan, stick with brown shoes. I'm a fan of anything leather or shiny on the feet. Get shoes that can be polished to look sharp. Don't wear a pair of shoes you wear every day or out to the clubs. Have one pair of interview shoes that you only wear on special occasions.

**Women:** I suggest a pump with a pointy-toe or round-toe with a high heel but not a super stiletto or platform. Remember, this is an interview not a Spice Girls audition. You want a shoe that looks trendy and fashionable but not too over-the-top. I'm not a huge fan of the kitten heel or flat shoe for the interview. Those are great for the workplace, but go a little fancier for the interview. Wear a pair of heels—you don't need to wear them every day. Keep the size of your heel down to four inches and under.

**Men:** Stay away from boat shoes or sneakers for an interview. Get a nice pair of oxfords or dress shoes, and make sure they match your suit.

## POP ACCESSORY

The pop accessory is a single colorful item that puts some personality in your look. As you all know, I'm not a fan of boring, so do your best to spice up your formal interview uniform.

**Women:** Add a trendy scarf, necklace, or chunky bracelet. Don't go too crazy as you want to keep the item tasteful. Stay away from oversized cocktail rings as they can come across as *too much*.

**Men:** The pop accessory is normally a tie. I spoke with Max Durovic, CEO of Aarrow Advertising, a San Diego–based company with an international virtual internship program. Durovic says, "The red tie is the power tie. But the light blue is a more subtle approach and communicates that you are a team player." When asked about ties to stay away from, Durovic says, "Stay away from ties with cartoon characters and excessively large knots at the top—ties that you would wear to a nightclub. Those aren't appropriate for the workplace. I'd also stay away from loud and flashy colors."[1]

## THE ALTERNATIVE INTERVIEW OUTFIT

Alyssa is a former intern of mine who attends the University of Kentucky in Lexington. We stay in touch and she keeps me up-to-date on her internship adventures. She was also an Intern Queen Campus Ambassador. Alyssa emailed me a few weeks ago with the following note:

Dear Lauren,

I am supposed to be meeting the owner of an event planning company for an interview this week. We are meeting at a Starbucks. My question is, what in the world do I wear? Since it isn't in her office I wasn't sure if I should really dress up. The outfit I had in mind was dark skinny jeans, black winter boots, a gray tank top with a black cardigan over it. Please let me know your thoughts! Thanks!

Alyssa[2]

I was so glad Alyssa asked about this because these seemingly casual or Starbucks interviews are becoming popular. The big red flags I saw in Alyssa's email were the words *jeans* and *boots*. Jeans aren't appropriate for interviews—even dark or black jeans. Khakis aren't appropriate either. They say, "I don't need to impress you."

Even though it's fancy for a Starbucks-like establishment, whip together your "alternative interview outfit." Please do not wear Ugg boots or clunky furry boots to an interview.

This was my message back to Alyssa:

Hi Alyssa,

Great question! It is very common (especially these days) for interviews to be at public coffee shops. Many entrepreneurs and employers who work virtually will do this—and sometimes executives just like to get out of the office for interviews. My advice is to go above and beyond. Most likely, the outfit you suggested would be fine BUT as you know, fine just isn't good enough for us. We always want to dress to impress, so I'd go a little fancier. I would suggest substituting the dark skinny jeans with a pair of black pants. I would also go with closed-toe heels over boots. I think the cardigan on top is fine. Again, we always want to dress up for that initial interview and then they will tell you what the dress code is for the internship. For all we know, the woman might have a thing against jeans.

Good luck. I know you will rock the house!

Best,
Lauren Berger
The Intern Queen

When putting together your alternative internship interview outfit I suggest the following two basics for men and women.

## THE CRISP, COLORED BUTTON-DOWN

You don't need to wear a jacket to a Starbucks-type interview. Wear a colored button-down since you won't have the jacket to put on top. Make sure you have the sweating situation under control as this can often be an issue for men and women when just wearing a button-down top.

**Men:** Tuck your shirt into your pants and don't feel the need for a tie for this type of interview. If you are wearing slacks, make sure you add a belt that matches. I say a colored top so you add some color and don't look blah. Are collared polo shirts acceptable? No, I'm going to say, "Too casual."

**Women:** Make sure to look neat and tuck your tops into slacks or into a pencil skirt to look sharp and sophisticated. An alternative to a button-down for females would be a short-sleeve version or a shell top (solid colored short sleeve or tank top). Make sure the top isn't see-through and you have no cleavage showing. Nice shells can be found at the Limited, Ann Taylor, H&M, and Macy's.

## DRESS BOTTOMS

**Men:** Wear dress pants or slacks and tuck your button-down into them. Stay away from jeans or khakis.

**Women:** As mentioned above, women can wear pants or a skirt. Just be careful with the skirts. Pencil skirts look great but you cannot wear one if it's too short. Make sure the skirt isn't too high above your knees, and if you are hesitant, go with a pair of pants; I would avoid dresses for interviews.

## ACCESSORIZING

The same rules apply for your alternative selection as far as dress shoes and a pop accessory for women. Men, make sure those socks match your suit and aren't white and sticking out.

## GROOMED AND POLISHED

Last week I had a big agency meeting in Beverly Hills. I wore a new suit jacket and did my makeup, but I didn't leave enough time to do my hair like I normally would. I was rushed and left the house before giving it another once over. After the meeting, I was excited and thought it went well. I looked to Michael, my business manager, and could tell something was bothering him. "Lauren, the back of your hair wasn't brushed. Do you think that makes you look good? It says sloppy all over it."

I felt terrible and stupid. And I knew Michael was right. If the agents noticed the hair issue, it may have cost me the meeting. Being well groomed is important in any situation. People want to know that you tried to put yourself together before you see them. My fingers are crossed that this won't be a problem when we follow up. My point is—you need to allow yourself enough time to get ready and make yourself look your absolute best for every interview.

**Men and women:** I hope I don't have to say floss and brush your teeth beforehand. If you know you are running around all day, stick a toothbrush and toothpaste in your car so you can run to the restroom right before the interview.

**Men:** This means shaving the day of the interview. And no dirt under your fingernails.

**Women:** If you're going with painted nails, make sure the coat is fresh without any nicks and avoid colors that scream, "I want attention." Don't let anything on your body overshadow your personality. No need for sparkles, acrylics that look clawlike, or different colors on different nails. Go out of your way to make them look nice. You don't need to get them professionally done, but they should look clean and presentable. A French manicure is always a safe bet.

Makeup should be kept to a minimum and shouldn't look like you caked it on for the occasion. Try the following advice for makeup:

- **Foundation and cover-up.** Make sure they match your skin tone. Ask the makeup counter at a department store to help you, if needed. If your skin type doesn't require you to wear foundation, you can leave it at home. Use cover-up to hide blemishes. Make sure your makeup is blended and doesn't have lines all over it. The best light in which to test your makeup color is natural light. Take a handheld mirror outside with you to ensure that you're perfectly matched and blended.
- **Light gloss on lips.** Lipstick comes across as heavy. Go for a light, neutral-colored gloss. The amount of lip gloss you wear on a date or a night out should not be worn to an interview. Keep it simple; don't distract the interviewer with tons of gloss.
- **Neutral eyes.** Eye shadows should be shades of brown or cream colors. Keep eyes very natural as your makeup should enhance your features and not take them over. Black or brown eyeliner and mascara are fine. No false eyelashes should be worn, and mascara should look natural and not over-the-top. Avoid what many makeup artists term "tarantula" lashes by limiting yourself to one clump-free coat of mascara.
- **Rosy cheeks.** If you like to wear blush, this can be great for interviews. Just add a touch; don't overdo it for an interview.

## What to Bring

Put together your internship interview kit. It should consist of the following:

- **Purse for women or briefcase/portfolio for men.** Women, your purses should be structured and professional looking. I suggest going all black and not bringing anything too stylish or trendy unless you are going to a fashion magazine interview. The employer must take you seriously, and your bag does make an impression. Men should also bring structured briefcases or sharp portfolios (these can be purchased at an office supply store).

- **Several blue or black ink pens.** You never know when you might be asked to sign paperwork. Having pens on you makes you look more prepared.
- **Notepad.** Have a decent-sized notepad with you, not a mini-memo pad. Make sure you have enough room to take notes, if asked. In fact, I encourage you to take notes if any important facts are stated during the interview. If the interviewer offers you the position on the spot and starts to go into detail about the position and lists any pertinent information, definitely take notes.
- **Well-kept copies of your resume and cover letter.** Bring copies of whichever documents you need to apply for the position, including any supplemental materials. Paperclip packets together with all of your information. Bring at least five copies of all materials with you as you never know how many executives will be in the meeting. When I say "well-kept," I mean bring materials that are clear, flat, and unwrinkled. Keep them in some sort of folder or portfolio so they stay sharp. I mentioned earlier in the book that you should print these materials out on a thick cream-colored paper so they don't feel too light. A nice thick paper stands out and shows more effort. Materials should be printed in all black ink.
- **Calendar.** If you have a handheld planner or calendar bring it. Otherwise, if you use the calendar on your phone, have your phone with you. Make sure your phone is on silent, of course.
- **Driver's license or photo ID.** This is usually needed to sign in at the front desk of an office building or to drive onto a studio parking lot.
- **Social security card.** It's not a bad idea to locate your social security card before an interview. If they hire you on the spot, they normally need a copy of your social security card to put you in their system.
- **Tide Pen or handheld stain remover.** Just in case you spill coffee on your white shirt before the interview, these small stain removers come in very handy.
- **Touch-ups.** Don't go into an interview with messy hair. Always look your best. If your interview is at the end of your day and you can't

stop home to freshen up first, stick a toothbrush, deodorant, and hairbrush in your car or bag.

## Miscellaneous Interview Tips and Advice

Here are a few other tips and advice as you prepare for your interview:

- **Arrive fifteen minutes early.** Planning on driving, walking, or biking to the office? Go there the day before the interview to make sure you know exactly how to get there. If you are traveling during heavy-traffic times, make sure you ask around (or check Google Map's traffic view) and find out what time you should leave for the interview. When you do your run-through the day before, try to travel at a similar time frame to get a sense of the traffic.
- **Watch your eating and drinking.** Try not to drink coffee or soda before the interview or eat too much. Drink water. This will also help prevent preinterview spills. Keep your teeth looking clean and white.
- **Be grateful and kind to everyone at the company.** Many businesses may have a valet or a doorman. You never know who these employees are friends with or what sort of pull they have at the company. If the interviewer is running late, don't be rude to the receptionist or roll your eyes. Executives are busy and often must squeeze in an interview at the last minute. Appreciate the time you get, as one solid interview can change your life.
- **Watch your posture.** Ladies, if you wear a skirt, make sure you know how to sit appropriately and keep your legs crossed. Guys, cross your legs at the knee or not at all. Don't sit with your ankle propped up on one knee—it gives the impression of a casual, disinterested attitude.
- **Sit still.** During the interview, try not to be fidgety. Avoid biting nails or twirling hair.
- **Speak confidently and at the appropriate volume and pace.**
- **Breathe.** Take a deep breath before answering questions so your remarks come out thoughtful and not rushed.

- **Avoid filler words.** When speaking professionally, avoid using words, such as *like*, that don't add to your vocabulary but distract from it. Similarly avoid "um," "ah," and other verbal stutters.
- **As my mother would say, "Look alive!"** The interviewer might be very monotone or seem disengaged, but make sure you stay attentive throughout the process. Often the employer goes into detail about the company or the position. Retain the information, smile, and nod to show you are listening.
- **If you bring a portfolio or work samples, ask the employer if he or she would like to look over your work.** Don't push your work in the employer's face or force him or her to look at it. Place all of your best work at the front of the portfolio as normally employers will only skim the first few pages.
- **Always thank the employer.** After the interview, thank the employer for his or her time, reach across and shake hands, and make eye contact. Simply state, "Thank you very much for taking the time to sit down with me today. I really appreciate it."

# AFTER-THE-INTERVIEW ETIQUETTE

Once the interview is complete, there are two things you must do. First, send the interviewer a handwritten thank-you note. Second, if you don't get a response after the interview and the employer hasn't mentioned a specific date when he or she will be in touch, send a follow-up email one week after the interview.

## Thank-You Cards

Thank-you cards are a must for after the interview. Handwritten thank-you notes are still very popular and mandatory in certain fields. You must snail-mail a thank-you note to the employer who interviewed you within two business days of the interview. I did not say "Send an email"—I said to send a handwritten thank-you note. I use personalized stationary that I reorder when my address changes. They are small cream-colored cards that say *Lauren Berger* in brick red writing at the top and have the same color red border. The cards are blank and simple and I can use them forever to send thank-you cards for interviews and gifts. You can print these types of cards up at any office supply or stationary store. If you cannot afford to get personalized stationary, purchase a pack of blank thank-you cards at the grocery or convenience store. Choose a box with a simple design on the front that says *Thank You* but is blank on the inside. Your thank-you card should say three things:

1. The purpose of the note is to say thank you for taking the time to sit down and do the interview. Acknowledge the employer's time as precious and valuable. Here's an example:

   Dear Ken Baker,
   Thank you so much for taking the time to sit down with me. I know you are extremely busy and appreciate your time.

2. Reference a discussion during the interview.

   I enjoyed hearing about your company goals for the new year and how interns play a strong role in the expansion of the business.

3. Include the next step you would like the employer to take, and properly close the note.

   I look forward to hearing from you soon.
   Best,
   Lauren Berger

I keep these thank-you notes and a sheet of stamps in my car so I can write them up right after the interview and stick them in the mailbox. This keeps the interview content fresh in my mind so I can reference it in the thank-you note.

# Follow-Up Notes

On your Intern Queen Dream List, I instructed you to leave a column available for follow-up. That column was in regards to the initial internship application. After the interview, you need to follow up as well. I suggest waiting one week after the interview to follow up with the employer if you haven't heard anything back. The follow-up can be in the form of an email or a call. When deciding which method to use, ask yourself, "What method has this person used the most frequently to communicate with me thus far?" For phone calls and emails, below is what you should say:

> Dear Ken Baker,
>
> I really enjoyed speaking with you last week. I wanted to follow up on the status of the internship. Please let me know if you'll need any additional materials. I look forward to hearing from you.
>
> Best,
> Lauren Berger

## 👑 INTERN QUEEN CHAPTER ESSENTIALS

- Understand the four types of interviews so that whenever one comes up, you are prepared.
- Always know where you can conduct a Skype interview. Ask your career center staff if they have webcams available for Skype interviews. If you have a webcam internally or externally on your computer, download Skype and video conference with friends and family to get a feel for how it works. Remember to create a professional Skype username.
- Respond to every employer's interview request within one business day. Tailor your response to each unique interview situation.
- Set aside time for company research. Go back to the company website, even if you've been there before. Review the company mission statement, *About Us* section, and google the company name for recent news tips.

- Make a list of your learning objectives for the internship after visiting the company website.
- Look up your school's career center online if you aren't familiar with its on-campus location. Call the center and schedule an appointment to do a mock interview. While you are there, also ask for a list of practice interview questions.
- Write down a few questions that you have for the employer based on your research.
- Prepare an appropriate outfit. Go through your closet and pick out the pieces that you already have that will work for the interview. Make a list of what you still need to go out and buy. Check discount stores first, as you will be surprised with the deals you can find these days on professional attire.
- Pack your interview bag with all of the must-haves (see the What to Bring section). Be sure to print out at least five copies of your application materials for each interview as you never know who will request a hard copy. Many times employers come to an interview unprepared, so it's helpful when you can hand them a fresh copy of your resume.
- Review the list of interviews tips, as you never know what you will forget to think about.
- Purchase thank-you notes. These can be on personalized stationary or blank cards from the convenience store. Make sure you have these ready to use after the interview.
- Make a note in your calendar of when you have your interview so you know the exact date on which you should be follow up (one week later).

Now that we've reviewed each type of interview and how to excel at each one, I'm hoping you'll feel relaxed and prepared for any situation. If you're still a little nervous, put that nervous energy to good use and rock the house! You already know you are wonderful and prepared, so convince the employer of that by letting your preparation show through. In the dating world, they say that one great date can change your life forever. The same adage applies to an interview: one great interview can change your life and your career path forever.

To reference my example from the beginning of this book, my initial interview at CAA paid off. After working for Tracy at CAA for two years, I learned more about the entertainment industry than I thought was possible as an entry-level employee. My professional contacts went from a few internship coordinators to an impressive list of actors, actresses, directors, publicists, managers, and agents. I understood how the industry worked from the inside out and felt confident that I could land any other desk in the entertainment industry after working for Tracy for so long. She taught me how to work, how to produce great material, how to execute ideas, and how to make things happen. Today I strive to run my business as Tracy runs hers—efficiently. She makes every day a busy and productive one. I am forever changed because of that position, and it will continue to positively affect my career. And to think, it all started with an interview.

## CHAPTER 6

# Let's Get
# **Legal**

One of my favorite internships was at a national television morning show called the *Daily Buzz*. The show tapes out of Orlando, where I spent my junior year at University of Central Florida. That year, the *Daily Buzz* brought on eight interns, and we had a slew of duties: maintaining the greenroom, welcoming guests, working closely under the show's directors and producers, assisting with segments, prepping the hosts, coordinating segments, and even appearing on the show. Before my internship, I knew nothing about television shows and how they were actually produced. This internship was especially challenging because I had to be in by 4 a.m. three days per week. I stayed from 4 a.m. until 10 a.m. while they filmed the show. My roommates would be going to sleep, and I'd be waking up for my internship. It was quite the experience!

One morning I was instructed to make coffee for the guests in the greenroom. It's a task some would call menial, but someone does need to make the coffee for the guests and keep them comfortable on a morning show. I walked into the break room that the *Daily Buzz* shared with a few other offices in the building. I looked at the coffee machine, honestly having no idea how to use it. I wasn't a coffee drinker at the time. The coffee machine was huge and had buttons everywhere, so I pressed one, not really knowing what would happen. Unfortunately I pressed the wrong button and coffee started spewing everywhere and flooding the break room floor. No one else was in the room. I started to panic and sprinted down the hallway to find someone who could help me. Clayton, an anchor of the show, was standing in the hallway and came to my rescue. We went back into the break room where people were standing and saying, "Who flooded the break room?" Clayton took the blame and helped me fix the coffee machine, clean up, and make a fresh pot for our guests. An internship is a time for you to learn, make mistakes, and fix them. If I started my first job at Creative Artists Agency (CAA) and didn't know how to make coffee, I would have been in trouble. Since I learned at my internship, I was prepared.

One of the reasons internships are controversial is because critics classify intern duties as mindless tasks. As you can see, everything has its place and even fetching coffee can be beneficial for students as long as that isn't what they spend the bulk of their time doing. Last year the *New York Times* published an article called "Unpaid Interns—Legal or Not?" that further explored the controversy within the internship space. Are unpaid internships illegal? What can students do to protect themselves at their internships? This article spurred debates among everyone involved with the internship equation—students, professors, parents, employers, and career coaches. Everyone took free rein to blast their opinions on internships.

Each year I visit colleges and universities worldwide and meet thousands of students energized by the subject of internships. They are driven, passionate, hard-working, and resilient in the face of any negative talk around the topic. They understand the value of real-world experience and building professional contacts—whether or not the work pays or is considered glamorous. They hear what critics say about internships being exploitative and termed "slave labor." But they keep going. They keep looking for opportunities. Although criticized for being part of a trophy generation and acting entitled, these students *want* to succeed and they want it bad. But until everyone shares this viewpoint on the power and importance of an internship, the controversy will continue.

The purpose of this book is not to pick sides or place blame, but to point out the guidelines that do exist. I teach students to walk into any situation prepared. To be prepared for an internship means understanding the rules in place to protect interns. I know you might consider this the *boring* chapter, but it's actually one of the most important. As a student, you should pride yourself on being informed. This will help you navigate your way through any unfair or uncomfortable situations that could potentially occur. I rarely hear about problems at internships, but they do pop up every so often. The best thing that you, the student, can do is be prepared. I'm calling this the *cautious* approach.

The majority of students and employers are unaware of the guidelines associated with internships. In this chapter, I aim to fix that and clearly explain each of the six criteria that legally define an unpaid internship. I also discuss issues involving sexual harassment in regard to paid and unpaid interns. The end of the chapter contains a list called "Your Rights as an Intern," which provides clarity and justification to students who are scared to speak up for themselves. To maintain a sense of transparency with my readers, I want to reiterate that I am not and will never claim to be a legal expert. Everything in this chapter is pulled from the US Department of Labor and EEOC's resources. The explanations provided are my translations of each rule to help students better understand what the guidelines say. And of course, laws change and different situations lead to different issues to consider, so if you have concerns or questions, you can always consult with a lawyer or human resources specialist. Knowing that, let's proceed and I'll walk you through exactly what you need to know to ensure you walk into every situation an informed intern.

# UNDERSTANDING THE FAIR LABOR STANDARDS ACT

The US Department of Labor (USDOL) created the Fair Labor Standards Act (FLSA) *Fact Sheet #71* to protect students from employers taking advantage of them and using them to substitute for actual employees. Keep in mind, the entire FLSA covers youth employment issues and is not limited to internships. The *Fact Sheet # 71* that I will be referencing throughout this chapter is titled *Internship Programs Under the Fair Labor*

*Standards Act.*[1] (If you want to refer to the complete document, you can view it at http://www.dol.gov/whd/regs/compliance/whdfs71.pdf. To find a link and pull up the FLSA, go to the United States Department of Labor website at dol.gov.)

To make sense of this document, I broke it down into sections and bulleted all of the important points that you should note. Before we begin, I want to explain that there is a distinct difference legally between the word *employ* and the word *intern*. Here is how those terms are defined in the FLSA *Fact Sheet #71*:

> *Employ:* To employ means to suffer or permit to work. Covered and nonexempt individuals who are *suffered or permitted* to work must be compensated under the law for the services they perform for an employer.
>
> *Intern:* Internships in the "for-profit" private sector will most often be viewed as employment, unless the test described below relating to trainees is met.

The "test" they refer to in the above definition of the word *intern* are the six criteria we are about to explore. For an unpaid internship to be legal, the opportunity must meet all six criteria. Just to clarify, these criteria are for unpaid interns. Paid internships do not need to abide by these.

## FLSA Point #1:

**The internship, even though it includes actual operation of the facilities of the employer, is similar to training which would be given in an educational environment.**

The internship must be a learning experience. Students should learn how a specific company is run and how to work in many capacities within that industry by listening, observing, and actually executing entry-level tasks. Each of those tasks must come with clear instruction and consistent supervision. Does this imply that you need to be watched like a hawk at all times? I should hope not, but employers must train you to complete tasks before assigning them.

Additionally each task must have a benefit for you, the student. Determine if the task you are given has a learning objective attached by constantly asking yourself, "What am I learning from this?" and "What will I get out of doing this task in the long run?" You can also ask yourself, "When might I use this skill in the future?" Writing down some of the tasks at your internship and what you are personally gaining from them will remind you what to include when updating resumes and preparing for interviews. I will explain this technique and how to write down learning objectives in chapter 8.

Let's say an internship coordinator is having you set up a Facebook page for their business. This helps you take what you already know about social media and apply it in a professional manner. Setting up and running a Facebook page is definitely something you could be asked to do as an entry-level employee, and knowing how to do this efficiently will help you with future career plans. If the Facebook page is successful, this will give you a success story to speak of during future interviews and will also give you social media experience to talk up in your cover letter.

## FLSA Point #2:

### The internship experience is for the benefit of the intern.

Notice this says the benefit of the *intern* and not the benefit of the *employer*. Unfortunately employers don't always understand this and use interns to do tasks directly related to generating revenue. Commonly this happens when interns act as salespeople and sell directly to clients. There is a big difference between an intern running a social media campaign that indirectly grows a brand and an intern selling directly to a client. To prevent this from happening, read over internship postings very closely. Be cautious of words like *sales, commissions,* and *making money.* Go with your gut instinct. Do you feel that your efforts alone are generating income for the employer? If yes, speak with your career center and get their opinion. Let them guide you on how to deal with this situation.

# FLSA Point #3:

**The intern does not displace regular employees,**
**but works under close supervision of existing staff.**

Point #3 also relates to an intern acting as an employee and generating revenue for the employer. Since 2009, we've seen an increase in layoffs nationwide. We must make sure that extra interns aren't brought on board to replace actual employees.

Mark Cuban, a famous businessman and controversial blogger, wrote a blog post where he expressed his frustration with the roadblocks he encountered when wanting to start a new organization within an existing company that was solely run by interns.[2] He thought it would be a great learning opportunity for students to create a brand. He ran this by his human resources department, and they told him he was not allowed to do that. Interns must be supervised, they cannot generate revenue, and they cannot replace actual employees. Mark Cuban's intentions were to provide students with an experience like none other, but this is where the FLSA rules come into play. Ask yourself, could the company run without me? If the answer is no, you have a problem you need to discuss with your career center as soon as possible.

# FLSA Point #4:

**The employer that provides the training derives**
**no immediate advantage from the activities of the intern;**
**and on occasion its operations may actually be impeded.**

The intern should be learning from the employer and assisting them, not doing their job for them. This point reiterates what we already covered and again says the intern shouldn't be directly generating revenue or participating in unsupervised activity. It also tells the employer that their operations might actually be "impeded" or slowed down because training an intern to do a task can be time consuming. You will notice many of the criteria are saying the same thing in different ways to protect the student.

# FLSA Point #5:

**The intern is not necessarily entitled
to a job at the conclusion of the internship.**

Periodically, *Bloomberg Businessweek* ranks their top fifty internship programs and lists their retention rates from intern to employee. Companies like PricewaterhouseCoopers retain close to 89 percent of their interns each year. IBM retains approximately 40 percent of their interns.[3] Several paid internships report retention rates, where the majority of unpaid internships do not report this information. Interns must understand that an internship in no way implies that a full-time job will be offered at the end. The internship should have a start date and an end date to show that it's not an open-ended opportunity. In chapter 9, I'll provide strategies for turning the internship into a full-time job. But it is important to walk into the internship knowing there might not be a pot of gold at the end of the rainbow—or, in this case, a job.

# FLSA Point #6:

**The employer and the intern understand that the intern
is not entitled to wages for the time spent in the internship.**

An internship is a two-way street, and when students start unpaid internships, they must completely understand that they are not entitled to any money under any circumstances at this position. During an interview, it is appropriate for a student to ask about wages or potential travel reimbursement. Once employers state that the internship is unpaid or paid and what they will or will not reimburse, the discussion is closed.

I want to be clear. If all of the six criteria mentioned above are met, the minimum wages and overtime laws do *not* apply and the position is therefore considered a legal unpaid internship. On the other hand, if you do feel that you should be paid, here is a link to information from the Wage and Hour Division on how to file a complaint: http://www.dol.gov/wecanhelp/ howtofilecomplaint.htm. You can also call their toll-free line for additional information at 1-866-487-9243.

# SEXUAL HARASSMENT IN
# THE WORKPLACE

The other major internship-related concern deals with sexual harassment in the workplace. In most instances, sexual harassment laws do not apply to interns as they are not considered employees. The only time that sexual harassment laws, as defined by the Equal Employment Opportunity Commission (EEOC), apply is with a paid internship at a company with more than fifteen employees. Otherwise paid interns at smaller companies and unpaid interns are not covered. However, there are still steps you can take to prevent this from happening and report it if it does. You can check here for the rules on coverage: www.eeoc.gov/employees/coverage.cfm.

First, let's discuss the legal definition of *sexual harassment*, as taken from the EEOC's website (www.eeoc.gov): "Harassment can include 'sexual harassment' or unwelcome sexual advances, requests for sexual favors, and other verbal or physical harassment of a sexual nature. Harassment does not have to be of a sexual nature, however, and can include offensive remarks about a person's sex. For example, it is illegal to harass a woman by making offensive comments about women in general."[4]

I spoke to Justine Lisser, senior attorney-advisor for the Office of Communications and Legislative Affairs at the EEOC, and she explained the two forms of sexual harassment. Keep in mind these apply to both men and women:

- Hostile work environment
- Quid Pro Quo (sexual favors as a condition of employment or an employment benefit), aka "I'll do this, if you do this"

Sexual harassment doesn't always happen with a boss or coworker; it can also happen with an outside customer or client of the business.[5]

# Dealing with a Hostile Work Environment

Meet Emily, a junior at Vanderbilt, interning at a large health care firm in Nashville for the summer. Emily has been an intern at the company for a few weeks and noticed one of her male coworkers, David, checking her out. Although she might have been attracted to him outside of the office, she wanted to keep things professional at her internship. David made frequent trips past Emily's cubicle and always went out of his way to say hello to her and ask what she was up to. He showed a clear interest in Emily's life, family, and daily activities at the company. One Thursday Emily got into the elevator at work to go downstairs and grab lunch, and David was in the elevator. He smiled as she walked into the elevator. She said hello and awkwardly stood with him in the elevator. David started whispering, "I want you. I want you." Emily felt uncomfortable and got out of the elevator as soon as the doors opened. From that day on, every time David would walk by Emily's desk he would mouth the words, "I want you." Emily didn't tell anyone what was happening for fear that she would get in trouble or it would get back to David that she reported him. She left the internship frustrated with the entire experience because of what happened.

This is what we would call a "hostile work environment," and it should be reported. Justine Lisser helped me put together two steps to take, should something like this happen:

1. **Make it clear that the person needs to stop.** "While it may sound obvious, the first thing anyone should do if they feel they are being harassed is to tell the person to knock it off. I appreciate that this may be difficult when it involves an unpaid intern being harassed by a person in power, but it may be sufficient to say: 'Mr. Smith, I'm here to learn about the company, not discuss what I do with my boyfriend with you,' or 'Jane, I appreciate that you have an informal workplace, but your requests to "get me alone to teach me a thing or two" make me very uncomfortable and I want it to stop.' Should things escalate, a very direct statement, 'Do not ever touch me again' is best."[6]

2. **Speak to someone.** Justine says, "If verbal requests to stop are insufficient, an intern should take his or her concerns to a supervisor of the person who is harassing him or her; the HR department, if the company is big enough to have one; the on-site intern coordinator, if there is one; or to anyone at his or her school who may have had some involvement in the intern process."[7]

Justine also warns that if a situation is dangerous, if physical assault is involved, physical safety is a priority even if it means walking out the front door of your internship.

In Emily's situation, she could have spoken to David about it, if she felt comfortable. And if she didn't feel comfortable, she should have spoken to the internship coordinator or human resources director at her company about what was happening. Another option would have been speaking with her career center about the problems and having them speak directly to the internship coordinator.

## Dealing with Quid Pro Quo

Now let's examine quid pro quo, the second type of sexual harassment. Below Justine Lisser provides an example of this situation and suggests steps students who are dealing with this should take:

1. **Document the actions.** Justine says, "The intern should document the actions, this can be in the form of a calendar notation: "Friday, August 3: Mr. Cookson, head of marketing, told me that there would always be a place for someone who knew 'how to put out' and that if I was 'nice' to him, he would be nice to me."[8]
2. **Complain and report.** The student should then complain to the same people noted above—supervisors, human resources, or internship coordinators.
3. **File a complaint with the EEOC.** When the intern is covered by the sexual harassment laws under the EEOC (paid interns at employers with over fifteen employees), a proper complaint should be filed.

To file a complaint, call 1-800-669-4000 or visit their website at eeoc.gov. Their website provides a list of EEOC offices throughout the country. Find the one closest to you. It is important to note that employment discrimination laws also protect against retaliation so that someone who complains should be protected from the employer taking adverse actions against an intern because he or she protested the sexual harassment.

## Preventing Sexual Harassment (to the Best of Your Ability)

Sexual harassment is never the student's fault. But again, let's do everything we can to prevent these types of situations from happening. Here are some things you can do to help prevent sexual harassment:

- **Dress appropriately.** Don't dress scandalously at your internship. Drawing attention to anything besides your shining intellect isn't appropriate in the workplace.
- **Stay professional.** There is always going to be that man or woman who hits on you at some point—inside or outside of the workplace. Just remember to ignore this type of inappropriate behavior and move on to the next thing. Give no signal of being on the same page as this person.
- **Remember the bigger picture.** You have an internship to move forward in your career, not to fall in love. In chapter 4 on social media, I introduced the everyone-knows-everyone mentality. This is no different in the workplace. You never know who the person trying to go out or hook up with you might be. Just like you don't want to burn any bridges, you don't want to take professional relationships too far. Impressions last and will follow you in your career.
- **What if you're in love?** Save it for after the internship. Your position is short term. If you want to discuss longer-term feelings with a coworker or employee, save that for when your internship has been completed.

# YOUR RIGHTS AS AN INTERN— FINALLY!

For this chapter, instead of generating a list of Intern Queen Chapter Essentials, I want to point out your rights as an intern. It's important to remember that you do have a voice when you feel you are being taken advantage of or sexually harassed at your internship. The Intern Queen brand is all about taking initiative and doing everything—everything, that is, *but* just standing there. If there is a problem, do something about it. If you don't, it could continue to affect students who walk in the door after you for years to come.

## Intern Queen's List of Student's Rights

- You have the right to accept an unpaid internship, providing it abides by the six criteria listed above.
- You have the right to learn something from each activity and task at your internship. But remember, even fetching coffee can be a learning experience, as that's what many entry-level careers entail. However, if *all* you are doing is getting coffee, you have a right to feel frustrated and take a stand. Schedule a time to speak with your internship coordinator and express your concerns about your daily tasks. Before you have this conversation, identify projects or departments you'd like to assist with.
- You have the right to ask questions about your tasks and about the workplace. Use your best judgment to decide when the most appropriate times to ask questions might be. If you tend to have several questions, try to put your thoughts together and ask them all at once to avoid a constant back and forth.
- If you are sitting around all day and not learning anything, you have the right to speak up and express your concerns to your direct boss at a prearranged time. I will speak more about this in chapter 8.

- Are you doing your employer's job for them? Do you feel like you are taking the place of an actual employee? You have the right to speak to the company HR department or your career center about the tasks you feel are inappropriate.
- If you aren't getting the proper instruction and feel thrown into tasks with little or no supervision, you have the right to discuss this with your career center or the HR department at the company. If you feel comfortable, you may also discuss this with your direct boss.
- You have the right to express interest in full-time career opportunities but cannot expect or assume anything will be given to you at the end of your internship.
- You have the right to ask to be reimbursed for travel or commuting-to-work expenses, but if you agree to an unpaid internship, you cannot expect any form of payment except experience (which can be worth a lot more than a couple bucks).
- If you are asked to sign any paperwork that you don't understand, you have the right to take your time, ask questions, and bring it to your career center to review.
- If you ever feel uncomfortable at your internship because of someone's actions, you have the right to ask them directly to stop or to report the matter to the HR manager or your career center. You do not have the right to start office gossip or talk poorly about anyone.

Now that you are familiar with the six criteria that define an unpaid internship and the sexual harassment laws affecting interns, you are ready to walk into your first day prepared. Like I said at the beginning of this chapter, you are informed and taking the "cautious" approach. I'm proud. You are well versed on the legalities behind internships so that, should you be put in an uncomfortable situation, you can feel confident in your ability to do something about it. In the next chapter, we'll discuss how to prepare for an internship and everything you will need for that first day. Remember, this internship will be life changing—get excited!

## CHAPTER 7

# Welcome to the
# **Internship**
# **Preparation**
# **Zone**

*You've got the internship—now what?* In this chapter, I answer that question and guide you through the logistics of your internship; the *who, what, where, when* and *why*. You need to arrive on the first day of your internship confident about *who* you will be working with, *what* to bring, *where* you are going, *when* to arrive, and *why* it's so important to be ultra-prepared. No one wants to walk into a situation feeling unprepared or overwhelmed. This chapter shows you how to prepare for every aspect of your internship and provides helpful resources for students planning on interning out of state or abroad. By the end of this chapter, you will be comfortable walking into any internship and confident that you will build a lasting impression from the first day onward.

# COMPANY LOGISTICS

We've all walked into new situations and felt shy or intimidated—it's perfectly normal. Prepare for your internship so that you do whatever you can to avoid feeling lost or uncomfortable. Here is a checklist to help you stay organized for the first day of your internship.

- ☑ **Company address.** Don't get this information online; make sure you confirm the address with the internship coordinator at least one week before you start your internship. Often online information is outdated, or the company has moved and the online address has yet to be changed. If you are going to a studio lot or major compound, you will need to ask what building you are going to.

- ☑ **Transportation.** Don't be afraid to ask the internship coordinator to recommend an easy route to get to the office from where you live. Obviously you can use Mapquest, Google, or GPS to check this information as well. I encourage you to do a practice drive, walk, or bus ride the day before just to make sure you know exactly where you are going and how long it will take to get there. Try to coordinate your travel time so that you experience the same amount of commuter congestion that you would on an actual internship day. This prevents you from pulling the "I was lost" card on the first day, which can give off a flaky impression.

- ☑ **Parking.** If you're planning on driving, make sure you ask where you are supposed to park and if you need a parking permit. If you need a permit, ask how to get one and how long that might take on the first day. You don't want to be late for your first day because you were held up in the parking office.

- ☑ **Where to Meet.** Where should you report on the first day? With whom will you be meeting? Know your contact's first and last names so that you can ask for him or her at security or the front desk. Also, have a contact number handy just in case you have problems. Make sure you know where to go once you get inside the building. Think about all of the details.

# Know the Key Players

Normally you can find the key executives for any business on the company website under About Us, Executive Team, or Bios. Read over the short biographies and credits for all of the executives listed. Familiarize yourself with their faces, if they have pictures, and read about how they got started and where they went to school. Try to locate similarities—this will come into play in the next chapter when we focus on networking. Print out a list of the key executives and try to memorize it. If you run into these people in the hallways, you aren't going to greet them by their titles (of course not!), but it can be helpful knowing who is around you. Whenever you run into this core group of executives, if appropriate, you always want to smile, say hello, and introduce yourself if you haven't met before. When I say "appropriate," I mean that if the executive is on the phone, in the middle of a conversation, or just looks like he or she doesn't want to be spoken to, save your introduction for a later date. If you are unsure of how to pronounce an executive's name, ask the internship coordinator. Tell the coordinator you were reading up on the company history and were curious. This can only help and make you look extra dedicated.

# Company Dress Code

In the interview section, we discussed the proper dress for interviews. Once you start the internship, understand what the company dress code is and abide by it. If you are unsure of the company dress code, ask the internship coordinator exactly what the company dress code reads. If you read over their instructions and are still not clear, ask the following questions:

- What are the ideal shoes to wear?
- Are jeans appropriate?
- Do men need a tie and jacket?
- Do men need collared shirts?
- Are sneakers allowed?

Notice I didn't put a question about flip-flops on this list because they shouldn't be worn even if they are allowed as you're trying to make a lasting impression. After all, the common expression is to "dress for the job you want, not the job you have." Keep in mind that some companies will send you home if you show up with inappropriate attire.

## What to Bring on the First Day

In chapter 5, I discussed what to bring for an interview. For your first day, the list is similar.

☑ Driver's license

☑ Social security card (If you don't have a copy, have your parents send you a photocopy.)

☑ A few pens that work (Stick with blue or black ink—no pencils.)

☑ Notepad (Get something decent sized so you can read what you've written down.)

☑ Snack bag (You never know when you will have a lunch break. Bring some pretzels or a granola bar to hold you over just in case you take a late lunch.)

☑ Mints (just in case)

☑ $15.00 (If the other interns are going out to lunch, you might want to join them. I encourage you to pack a few lunches to save money, but on the first day, you might want to eat out with everyone else.)

☑ Folder (Most likely, you will be handed paperwork on the first day. Have an appropriate place to put it.)

☑ Laptop (Ask your employer ahead of time if you need to bring a laptop with you. Normally the answer is no. However, if you are interning at a small business or start-up, they might have you bring your own computer.)

# What to Expect on the First Day

Usually companies with large-scale internship programs do internship orientation on the first day. At an internship orientation session, you learn about the company policies, procedures, intern tasks, intern events, and get advice from the staff on how to make the most of your internship. Midsized and small businesses often take a few minutes to provide a brief overview and answer any questions, then put their new interns right to work.

Expect to take lots of notes on the first day. Every time an employer asks you to do something or calls you into his or her office, bring your pen and notepad. This shows you are taking everything very seriously. Make notes on everything, even the information that seems trivial, as this is what you'll be first to forget. Unfortunately there can be lots of down time for the first few days of the internship. Battle this by reading everything you can get your hands on—trade publications, press releases, old company promotional material. Whenever you find yourself with nothing to do, ask the internship coordinator if you can help with a project. If the internship coordinator doesn't need help, ask if you are allowed to go around and ask other executives if they need assistance. Establish yourself quickly as the "go-to" intern whenever someone needs something.

Be ready to ask lots of questions. You will be in the workplace for the first time—or if you've had previous internships or part-time jobs, you'll be in a new workplace with different surroundings, policies, and company culture—and it isn't something to take lightly. Absorb and write down what you can. As tasks get assigned, make a list of all of your questions. When the tasks have been explained to you, ask your questions if they haven't already been answered.

If your internship program includes fellow interns, you'll also meet them on your first day. Be prepared to love some and not like some—such is life! Be the intern who plans intern social activities and keeps everyone tied together (there is always one). This way you gain everyone's contact information and make sure to constantly build and strengthen relationships. Remember to stay in close contact with all of the other students you meet at your internships; you never know when one of those connections could help you—or them—in the future!

# COMMUNICATION RULES FOR INTERNS

As an intern, you are learning to communicate in a professional setting, most likely for the first time. Expect a learning curve, as you quickly learn that the workplace is filled with several types of personalities: from extroverts to introverts, type A to type B. My advice is to slide in somewhere in the middle. Be the intern who caters to every type of personality by listening and really making an effort to identify with these different individuals and get a good sense of their personality. If you are extremely extroverted (like me), you might need to tone that down a bit when around an employee who seems to be more introverted and vice versa.

When I started an internship the summer before my senior year of college, I was overly eager to start my position. I sent the internship coordinator (we'll call her Heather) about twenty emails leading up to the first day. I told Heather how excited I was to start and would ask her any question that popped into my head. I thought I was being prepared. Summer arrived and I moved to Los Angeles to start my internship. When I met Heather on the first day, I was overjoyed and gave her a huge hug. Heather didn't seem too excited to see me, but I brushed it off, convinced I was reading too much into it. Over the next few weeks, I learned that Heather had decided she didn't like me before I started the position. She found my constant emails super annoying and had already formed an opinion about me. Even though Heather didn't seem to enjoy my personality, other executives did. They often invited me to sit in on meetings. Now, Heather was an assistant at the company for one of the executives who took an instant liking to me. Heather was trying to work her way up the corporate ladder. Whenever I'd walk into a meeting, I'd have to pass Heather's desk. I couldn't help but notice the glare on her face every time I'd walk into a meeting. I didn't understand the problem. In fact, it took me almost a month to realize what was going on. Heather was jealous. Her boss never invited her to meetings. Instead, the random summer intern (me) was invited into meetings. Because of this, Heather didn't like me and assigned me the work that no one else wanted to do.

At an internship, you are expected to manage a variety of different relationships with no formal training. How do you interact with an internship coordinator, a fellow intern, a boss?

Below I've included different advice for different types of relationships.

## Student and Executive-Assistant Internship Coordinator

This relationship is rarely explained to a student before the internship. In industries where the executive assistant often serves as the internship coordinator (entertainment, public relations, new media, marketing), an unspoken tension exists between the student and the internship coordinator (like the one between Heather and me). The student gets the internship and then harasses the internship coordinator (without realizing it) by sending a different email each day asking a different question about the opportunity. When communicating with an internship coordinator, pause, and put all of your questions into one large email. An internship coordinator has plenty of other tasks (especially at small businesses where they don't hire stand-alone coordinators) and doesn't think about the interns all day. The coordinator certainly doesn't want to be bombarded with too many emails before the internship starts. Remember, many times these assistants or midlevel executives are trying to work their way up the ladder at that company. Over the summer, the intern comes on board and gets a significant amount of attention. The internship coordinator feels threatened and may change the way he or she treats the student. Be aware of this issue and do everything you can to make sure that internship coordinator knows you are there to learn and not to steal his or her job. Also, keep in mind that the internship coordinator might only be a few years older than you or could even be your age. In some cases, the internship coordinator could be younger than you. Make sure that you stay professional and don't forget the coordinator is your boss, not your friend. Make sure you always volunteer for everything, arrive on time, and don't be caught on your cell phone or using Facebook. Through your hard work and attentiveness, show the coordinator that this internship is your number one priority.

## Intern and Boss or High-Level Executive

You and the internship coordinator will have a somewhat informal relationship since you will work together daily. However, if the internship coordinator is also the big boss, this is another story. Be as formal as possible when dealing with the head of the department or company. Listen very carefully on the first day and always ask how you should be communicating with the boss. Perhaps he or she prefers to be emailed questions instead of called—or updated over Skype rather than email. Clarify this with your boss on the first day to show that you respect his or her time and preferences. Also, it's appropriate to say on the first day, "If I have questions, who should I ask?" Let your boss dictate the chain of command so you never have to question this. Always address your boss by Mr. or Ms. or Mrs. (or Dr.) unless he or she corrects you and tells you to call him or her something else. Make sure that you knock on the boss's door before walking in and always ask permission to speak before launching into a conversation. Stay formal and let the boss determine how casual your relationship will become.

## Intern to Intern

You won't like everyone you intern with. Sometimes a student gets an internship because his or her father is head of the company or some other personal connection. In life, everyone deals with this. Don't treat this person any differently as he or she is still a great contact for you. Your job is to build your network. Communicate with your fellow interns as you would communicate with friends. But keep in mind, professionals are around you. There is no need to speak loudly about crazy weekend parties, girlfriends, boyfriends, or anything personal. Keep the social talk for lunch time or after the internship.

## Phone Etiquette

Interns are commonly asked to answer phone calls for an executive or for a company. Most likely the company will train you on exactly how to answer its phones. Just remember to always be as professional as possible to the person with whom you are speaking. You might be answering the phone for the company's biggest and highest paying client, and you cannot afford to be rude, even if the person on the phone is offensive. Use the old "kill them with kindness" rule.

I hope I don't have to mention that cell phones are not allowed at your internship. Keep them in your pocket, car, or purse and on silent—not vibrate. Don't give your colleagues the impression that you have better things to do.

## Social Media Etiquette

At select companies, interns run marketing and press campaigns over Facebook and Twitter. If the company tells you to spend time on your Twitter page or work on the company Facebook group or fan page—that's fine. Otherwise, you shouldn't be on social networks during your internship. If anyone sees you on those networks, you will quickly become "that guy who was on Facebook" or "that girl who was on Twitter." Don't forget that you worked hard to get the internship, so you may as well put 100 percent into it. Remember, the second you have nothing to do at your internship, get up out of your chair, and ask the internship coordinator if he or she needs help. If that person doesn't need help, ask other executives if they need help.

# RESOURCES FOR OUT-OF-STATE INTERNSHIPS

Traveling to a location outside of where you live or go to school for an internship is very popular. New York City is the most popular summer internship destination followed by other major metropolitan cities like Los Angeles; Washington, DC; Chicago; and Miami. Interning abroad is also a growing trend. Students aren't just going abroad to study; they are going abroad to intern. Below I get into detail about where to stay and how to organize your internship travels. Have fun and good luck!

## New York

I went to New York City to intern the summer after my freshman year of college. I interned for *Backstage*, the theatre trade publication. I walked to work every day from Hayden Hall, the NYU dorm to which I was assigned in Washington Square Park. Over that summer, I met people who remain close friends to this day. I wouldn't trade that summer for the world.

Each summer students from all over the world come to New York City to intern with the employers of their dreams. New York is an exciting summer internship destination but can also feel overwhelming if you don't have the right logistics in place. Below are some housing resources you might find helpful. The housing choices for students coming from out of state or abroad fill up fast. I suggest booking these prior to March for the summer internship season.

### COLLEGE DORMS

Several universities in New York City, including those in the list below, open their dorms to nonstudents over the summer as a way to generate extra income. Pricing varies, so check the websites for current pricing details.

Columbia University Summer Housing
http://housingservices.columbia.edu/content/intern-housing-2011

Fordham University Summer Housing
www.fordham.edu/Academics/Summer_Session/

Long Island University Summer Housing
www2.brooklyn.liu.edu/housing/LIUSummerInternApplication.pdf

New School University Summer Housing
www.newschool.edu/studentservices/housing/summer-housing/

NYU Summer Housing
www.nyu.edu/summer/housing/

Personally I can vouch for the NYU program. My parents felt safe with me at an actual college dorm that had security downstairs, roommates, and other interns buzzing around town. I was able to get on the NYU meal plan and also use their fitness center. I highly recommend looking into all of these live-on-campus opportunities.

## OTHER NYC HOUSING OPTIONS

There are several other organizations (both for-profit and nonprofit) that open their doors to summer interns. Please remember to check into these places ahead of time and make sure they are centrally located and will provide a safe environment for the summer. Here are a few places that cater to summer interns:

EHS (Educational Housing Service)
www.studenthousing.org/what-we-offer/interns

NYC Intern
www.nycintern.org

Webster Apartments (for women only)
www.websterapartments.org

## CORPORATE HOUSING

In addition to college dorms, I've stayed in corporate housing. I do have to warn you, however, that if you stay alone, it gets pricey. If you find a roommate, these situations become more affordable. Normally with corporate housing, your furniture and amenities (towels, bedding) are supplied.

National Corporate Housing
www.nationalcorporatehousing.com

Oakwood Corporate Housing
www.oakwood.com

# Los Angeles

I interned in Los Angeles for two summers in a row. The first summer I went on craigslist.org and found a sublet. My dad spoke to the girl on the phone ahead of time to evaluate the situation and give his approval. My dad flew out to Los Angeles with me just to make sure everything was safe. My roommate, Diem, was amazing, and we are still friends today. Diem rented a two bedroom/two bathroom in West Hollywood, and my friend Ashley and I split the price of the sublease on the second bedroom for the months of June and July. The summer was amazing, and I had a comfortable and centrally located place to call home.

Los Angeles isn't the easiest place to intern because the public transportation system isn't as widely used or practical as other metropolitan areas. If you don't have a car, it can be extremely difficult to get around. I didn't go to Los Angeles through a school program. I went on my own both summers. The second summer in Los Angeles, I stayed at the Oakwood Corporate Housing. However, if you stay focused and determined, you can make your summer in Los Angeles a great internship experience.

## SUBLETS IN LOS ANGELES

Because not as many schools open their doors to nonstudents in the Los Angeles area, housing can be a bit tricky. I suggest looking into sublets since there are so many universities in the area and plenty of students go home for the summer and love subletting their apartments. Check out these resources for student sublets:

- **craigslist.org.** We all know about craigslist. Just be careful.
- **ULoop.com.** ULoop helps college students find subletters for the summer. Check this site out and see if you can find something of interest in the area where you want to intern. My Northwestern University Intern Queen Campus Ambassador, Meredith, just accepted a summer internship at United Talent Agency in Los Angeles. She used this site to find a sublet from a USC student who was traveling home for the summer.

## CORPORATE HOUSING

Just like New York, Los Angeles has several corporate housing facilities. The most popular for summer interns is the Toluca Lake destination of the Oakwood.

National Corporate Housing
www.nationalcorporatehousing.com

Oakwood Corporate Housing
www.oakwood.com

## SCHOOL PROGRAMS

Several colleges and universities have "Semester in L.A." programs or other alternative programs where students can study or intern in locations outside of where the school is based. Find out if your school has a program specific to internships by asking at the career center, field work office, film studies program, or student services. These programs are great as they offer valuable experience and the chance to bond with your classmates. Some of the colleges and universities with popular semester-in-L.A. programs include:

Boston University
Columbia College (Chicago)
Elon University
Emerson University
Ithaca College
Syracuse University

University of Central Florida
University of Illinois—Carbondale
University of Texas at Austin
Vanderbilt University

## Washington, DC

Washington, DC, is a very popular internship destination. The DC intern scene is flooded with political interns over the summer. Here are a few internship housing options for students planning to intern in DC in summer:

## COLLEGE DORMS

American University Summer Housing
www.american.edu/ocl/housing/intern-housing.cfm

Georgetown University Summer Housing
http://housing.georgetown.edu/summer/index
.cfm?fuse=overview&type=nongu

The George Washington University Summer Housing
www.summerhousing.gwu.edu

## ALTERNATIVE SUMMER HOUSING OPTIONS FOR STUDENTS

The Washington Intern Housing Network
http://thewihn.com

Washington Intern Student Housing
www.internsdc.com

## Resources for Interning Abroad

If you plan on interning abroad, I suggest you go through a program that specializes in internships abroad and takes a large group of students every year. I suggest this for safety reasons and so you have a big group of students your age to become friendly with and to travel around with. Here are a few programs that specialize in these opportunities:

AIFS Program
http://aifsabroad.com

Bunac Program
www.bunac.org

CDS International
www.cdsintl.org

Accent Study Abroad Program
http://accentintl.com

GoAbroad
www.goabroad.com

## International Students Coming to the United States to Intern

Students traveling to the United States from other countries often ask about the internship process. What do they need to do if they want to intern in the United States? Here are a few quick tips:

- **Apply for the internship.** US employers will look over your information. Use your cover letter to really connect the dots and tell the employer your situation and make it seem as effortless from their end as possible.
- **Get your visa squared away.** Different countries have different policies as far as student visas are concerned. Do your reading in advance if you plan to intern in the United States. I encourage you to start looking at the visa guidelines eight to fifteen months before your desired start date. The best resource for this is on the US Department of State website, http://travel.state.gov/visa/temp/types/types_1268.html. Certain visas require that you provide several different items including school transcripts, standardized test scores, and bank statements. Again, these requirements are different for each country, so make a checklist of everything you need.

---

☑ **Get a passport.** Passports can take a few weeks to process. You want to get your passport at least three months in advance, if at all possible.

☑ **Know your time frame.** The National Homeland Security allows international students to enter the United States only thirty days (or less) prior to the start date of the internship. Note that several additional "special" permits do exist, if needed. See the US Department of State website, noted above, for information.

☑ **Practice your English.** The more English you know, the easier the transition will be. Practice makes perfect!

☑ **Get excited!** This is something you can definitely do if you set your mind to it. Any company in the United States would be lucky to have such an ambitious student. Keep going!

---

# Tips for Interning Out of State

Since I've personally interned out of state on multiple occasions, I have a list of tips that I wish someone had told me before I took on these out-of-state opportunities.

## TRANSPORTATION

In New York and Washington, DC, you won't need a car. Be prepared to walk to your internship or take the subway on a daily basis. Definitely pick up a free map of the subway system and learn your way around the neighborhoods where you live and work. As I mentioned earlier in the chapter, do that practice walk or subway ride to work before your first day. An umbrella is definitely something you will want to put in your bag. Ladies, when purchasing or packing shoes for your internship, be aware that you might have to do intense walking in them. Many female executives in New York City walk to work in sneakers or flip-flops and change into more professional footwear once they arrive at the company—this isn't a bad idea for you as well.

In Los Angeles, you will probably need a car to get to and from your internship each day. Unlike New York City, Los Angeles is extremely spread out, and it takes approximately twenty minutes to get from one side of the city to the other when there is no traffic. Since Los Angeles is known for traffic, it normally takes closer to forty-five minutes to get where you want to go. I shipped my car from Florida to Los Angeles two summers in a row. One summer the shipping company brought my car back to Florida with nothing in the trunk. I had packed my trunk full of clothing and my desktop computer beforehand. I don't know who stole all of my things out of my trunk. But be careful. If you do ship your car, don't put anything in your trunk, even if it seems like an easier way to move your stuff at the time. Other options are renting a car or taking public transportation. If you are interning in Los Angeles with a school program, they might have a bus that drops each student off at his or her internship each morning.

# Packing List for Interning Out of the State or Country

Most internships last for approximately ten weeks. This packing list is based on a summer internship in a warm climate. Remember, I'm only providing you with suggestions for the internship portion of this. It's up to you to remember to pack your undergarments, play clothes, and other necessities.

## LADIES' IDEAL PACKING LIST: INTERNSHIP CLOTHING

☑ Three long-sleeved button-down tops. These can go under suit jackets, get tucked into skirts, or even be worn with jeans on a casual day. I suggest one white button-down and the others in versatile colors for mix and match purposes (grays, neutrals, black, baby blue).

☑ One black knee-length or pencil skirt (of the appropriate length). Pack something basic that you can rotate into your internship wardrobe easily.

☑ Two pairs of work pants (aka dress pants or slacks). I suggest black and dark charcoal as they'll work with everything.

☑ One pair of workplace-appropriate jeans to wear on casual Fridays or summer Fridays. These shouldn't have holes, patterns, or frayed edges.

☑ One black or dark-colored suit. Even if you don't need one for your internship, this is good to have if you are invited to an event.

☑ Two work dresses. Bring two dresses that have sleeves and can be worn in the workplace. Since you are only bringing two of them, feel free to make them standout dresses. They don't have to be basic, but make sure they're not too wild for the office.

☑ Two cardigans of any color. Make them fun colors. As you already know, these are great to throw on and they make any top (for the most part) appropriate for the workplace.

☑ Three basic blouses or tops that have sleeves and are appropriate for the workplace. These should be nice tops that you can wear under your business suit, with a skirt, or with dress pants. They can have patterns or some color to them, but avoid anything too extreme. You want to be able to rewear these items without people taking much notice.

☑ One black tank top shell. This is to go under a buttondown or your business suit and will just come in handy.

☑ One white tank top shell. Again, this will go with everything and be a handy piece to own.

☑ One skinny belt. The belt can be black, brown, red, or whatever you want. This will be a go-to accessory for tons of internship outfits.

☑ Two pairs of workplace shoes, one black, one brown. Purchase smaller wedge heels so they aren't difficult to run around in.

# MEN'S IDEAL PACKING LIST: INTERNSHIP CLOTHING

☑ Two suits. You want to have some sort of rotation going on. Even if these aren't needed for the internship, make sure you have one for special events. (You never know!)

☑ Seven ties. If you are going to be at this internship for approximately ten weeks you want to have some nice ties so you don't look like you are wearing the same thing every day. If you know the dress code does not require a tie, bring one or two so that you have an option for a fancy event, should you be invited to attend a work or social function.

☑ Seven dress shirts. Remember, many of these can double as "going out" shirts for night time. Just in case there is a laundry failure, you should have one full week's worth of clean shirts!

☑ Two belts. Bring one black, one brown, or one reversible!

☑ Dress Socks. Pack at least ten pairs to last you two weeks just in case you have laundry issues.

☑ Two pairs of dress shoes. Bring one black and one brown.

☑ Four pairs of dress pants or slacks. I suggest one khaki pair and one gray pair for days that you don't feel the need to be as formal. The khakis are the least formal, so do not wear them unless you know it's okay.

☑ One pair of workplace-appropriate jeans to wear on casual Fridays or summer Fridays. These shouldn't have holes, patterns, or frayed edges.

☑ Two nice collared shirts. These shirts can be short sleeved as long as they look pressed and not old and junky.

And like magic—you are prepped, packed, and ready for your destination internship!

# 👑 INTERN QUEEN CHAPTER ESSENTIALS

As we reach the end of this chapter, ask yourself, do I feel prepared for this internship? Go back through some of this chapter and make sure you've done all of the following:

- Made a list of the company logistics: address, parking, directions, where you are going, and who you are meeting with
- Gone to the company website and looked at the bios for the executives and read through them. You have an idea of who's who at that company.
- Asked the internship coordinator about the company dress code policy
- Reviewed the list of what to bring on the first day and checked off all of the items
- Looked over all of the communication rules between you and the internship coordinator, boss, and fellow interns

- Understood the proper phone and social media etiquette for your internship
- Reviewed the suggested resources and looked over the packing list suggestions for the duration of your internship if you plan on interning out of state or overseas.

I'm sure by now you get it—preparation is key. You will be the intern who is always prepared and never forgets to bring things or write information down. Your organization skills are going to shine, and the employer is going to notice your readiness and preparation. Remember, I've been in your shoes. I was once an intern who was usually not prepared for my internships. I wish that someone had provided me with all of this information. It would have saved me lots of time, energy, and embarrassment. No matter where you are in your internship process today, bookmark this section, as I promise you will want to come back to it once you are ready to start your internship. Once you read this entire chapter, it should provide you with a sense of confidence. In the next chapter, we will get into the actual internship—what to expect and how to knock the employer's socks off. Because let's be honest—that's what you're going to do!

## CHAPTER 8

# On-the-Internship
# **Advice**

The summer before my junior year of college, I interned at BWR Public Relations, a celebrity publicity firm located in Beverly Hills. At BWR every Friday was called "summer Friday," and the interns sat in for the assistants while the assistants got the day off. Meanwhile, the interns learned how to *roll* calls (as they say in Hollywood), email professionals, and schedule meetings. We all looked forward to Fridays and thought we were so cool when we got to take over an assistant's desk for the day. One summer Friday, I was covering a desk and I saw a business card on the floor. Now whose name was on that business card? Ken Baker! Ken Baker is currently the head of E! News. But at the time, Ken Baker was the West Coast editor of *Us Weekly* magazine. If you remember from chapter 1, *Us Weekly* magazine was my dream job. I had a few options. I could have left the business card on the floor or put it on one of the executives' desks. Perhaps I could have thrown it away? I decided to take a risk. Throughout my internship journey, I learned that you must tell people what you want to do. I emailed Ken Baker and introduced myself:

> Dear Ken Baker,
>
> I found your business card on the floor at my internship. *Us Weekly* is my dream company to work for. I'd love to be an intern, reporter, or writer. I'm transferring to University of Central Florida in August. The school is located

in Orlando, Florida—where I know several celebrities visit. Please let me know if you have any advice, as I'd love to work for *Us Weekly*.

Best,
Lauren Berger

I sent this email over the summer and didn't hear anything back for months. Finally, in November, I was at home with my family for Thanksgiving and the phone rang.

"Hey, Lauren! This is Ken Baker calling from *Us Weekly* magazine. Are you still interested in freelancing for us? We have a story for you to cover in Orlando!"

I couldn't believe it.

"Ummm . . . yes! I'd love to."

My first assignment was to cover a Justin Timberlake and Cameron Diaz sighting in Orlando. I ended up freelancing for *Us Weekly* throughout my junior and senior year of college. I was not an intern for them; I was a reporter and got paid—well! For *Us Weekly*, I traveled the country and received several bylines (mentions) in the actual publication. They even published my photo once!

The best thing you get out of your internship is contacts. It's critical to understand how to build these relationships and make them last as these may be the people who help you land your first job. The way you will build these contacts is by knowing exactly how to impress the employers at your internship. It's also important to understand how to deal with conflict in the workplace to ensure you don't burn any bridges.

This chapter covers the best part of the internship process—the actual experience. I include networking tips, pointers on how to best work with employers and impress the entire office, and how to deal with different types of conflict at your internship. You never know what might happen at your internship. Going into this year, you must take action and tell people what you want to do with your life. No one will do it for you. Use your internship as a springboard to your future.

# NETWORKING 101

At your internship, you are in front of several potential employers within that company. Here's how to make them notice you—you start by introducing yourself.

## Introducing Yourself

It's your job to make sure everyone in your department knows who you are. If you are at a small or midsized company, you might be able to let the entire company know who you are. Normally the internship coordinator or human resources director will take you around the office on your first day, introducing you to important executives or people you'll be working with. However, this doesn't always happen; it depends on the company and its internship program. If you do get walked around the office, pay close attention to everyone's name. Greet people by their names as often as possible—when you see them in the hallway, break room, or front lobby. Of course, you will refrain from doing this if they are speaking with someone else, on the phone, or just look like they don't want to be bothered.

If you don't get walked around the office, take it upon yourself to make the introductions. Anytime you are pouring a cup of coffee, in an elevator, break room, or wherever—introduce yourself. Again, the only time you wouldn't do this is if the employee is on a call or speaking with someone else. When introducing yourself, reach out your hand, provide a firm handshake, look the person right in the eyes, and state your first and last name. You don't want to be one of the seven Ashleys from upstairs. In chapter 9, I'll discuss how a strong introduction and networking with multiple individuals in a company can lead to a full-time job offer.

## Creating Deeper Relationships

I have about ten friends whom I consider my closest friends. We speak a few times per week and know almost everything about each other's lives.

We talk about relationships and problems and constantly provide advice for one another. Our relationships are anything *but* surface or fake.

Now, when I look at my Facebook friends or think about some of my old coworkers, the relationships are more surfacelike. If I run into one of them while I'm out, we say hello, talk about work and the weather, and give one another casual updates—and then it's done. Usually we say we should get together sometime and never do. And that's fine—they are *those* kinds of relationships.

Employer relationships should be somewhere in the middle. You want to become comfortable speaking with these individuals so that you have more to talk about than just your career. The goal is to learn what's important to each of your professional contacts. Some executives speak about their spouses, children, or pets all day, whereas other executives are legitimately obsessed with clients and their work. Understand what drives each of these people so that you can build deeper relationships with them.

Approach executives standing alone in the break room, elevator, or hanging around your cubicle before a meeting. Start with a simple, "How are you today?" and then you can add, "I'm Lauren Berger, one of the summer interns; what was your name?" You don't need to find out the person's entire life story on the first meet-and-greet. Continue to say hello in passing, and the next time you are in an environment where you can chitchat, ask the person how his or her weekend was or about any plans for the following weekend. The goal is to build a relationship so the person is comfortable speaking with you during free time around the office.

## Organizing Your Contacts

Every time you meet new professional contacts, you must write down their names immediately. If they don't give you a business card, it's usually easy to figure out their email address. Look at other executives' email addresses, and use the same protocol. For example, at Network X everyone's email might be firstname.lastname@networkX.com, so when you meet new people, it's easy to write down their email addresses. Most large corporations also have all of their employees on an internal database, so you can double-check the spelling of the person's name. I suggest you create an Excel document on your personal computer to keep track of the contact's first name, last name, email, phone number, company, and a note reminding yourself of how you met. While at your internship, track your new contacts in a notebook and then transfer them to your computer when you get home. These are the people you will reach out to at the end of your internship to thank them for the opportunity you had to work with them.

## Setting Informational Meetings

At my FOX internship, my fellow intern Rob and I decided we wanted to meet every executive on our floor. We were interning in the drama development department and were on the same floor as the vice president of the network, the head of publicity, the head of scheduling, and the head of programming. And of course—we wanted to meet them all! We sent emails to all of the executives:

> Dear (First Name, Last Name),
>
> We are currently interning in the drama development department on your floor. Our internship lasts until the beginning of August. We'd love to meet with you before that time and hear about how you got started and get advice for our own careers.
> We know you are really busy and would appreciate any time you can offer. Please let us know what might work for your schedule.
>
> Best,
> Lauren Berger (UCF) & Rob Forman (Penn)

Rob and I sent this email out to a total of ten executives and seven of them wrote back to say we could meet with them. We ended up sending the email to executives on our floor who we admired. We were ecstatic about the response! We scheduled meetings with their assistants and were able to have five to ten minutes of their attention—just for us. The best part of these meetings was that at the end, the executives would hand us their business cards and say, "Please stay in touch." And just like that—another contact was made.

To properly set informational meetings of your own, follow these steps.

## STEP 1: DETERMINE WITH WHOM YOU WANT TO MEET.

You can set informational meetings whenever you want. You don't have to be an intern at the time. While you are a student, milk the student card as much as possible. Executives will take the time to sit down with you and tell you how they got started and what advice they have to share (those are the key phrases to use). Remember, not everyone will be positive; some will ignore your email or just say no. But no matter what, keep trying and reach out to more people. Make a list of approximately twenty people that you'd like to meet with (at your internship or just in general). If you want to meet these people in person, they should be in the city where you intern, live, or go to school. If you are requesting phone calls, they can be located anywhere.

## STEP 2: WRITE OUT YOUR NOTE

This should be done via email. Notes should be short and just a few sentences with a call to action at the end. An example would be ending with "Please let me know when we might be able to schedule a call or meeting over the next few weeks."

## STEP 3: HAVE A MINI-AGENDA

More than likely, this will be a five- or ten-minute meeting and no longer. Make sure you identify specific questions to ask the employer. Ask yourself beforehand, what do I want to leave the conversation with? Good questions to ask include these:

- How did you get started in the business?
- Knowing that I want to do [insert potential career choice], what path do you suggest I follow?
- What are your pointers for making the most of my internship at this company?
- What materials should I be reading or aware of to succeed in this industry?

- Are there any networking events or professional groups you suggest I become part of?
- Is there anyone else in this company or outside of the company that you think I should meet with to continue growing my perspective on the industry?

### STEP 4: GO IN PREPARED

Go into these meetings with pen and paper handy. If the employer provides names of books you should get, websites you should check out—write this stuff down. It shows you take yourself and your career very seriously.

### STEP 5: CLOSE IT PROPERLY

If the person doesn't end the meeting by handing you a business card, make sure you say, "What is the best way to stay in touch with you?" Thank the person for his or her time at the end of your meeting.

# TIPS FOR MAKING THE MOST OF YOUR INTERNSHIP

Sometimes it may feel like you are jumping through hurdles to land the actual internship and once you start, you lose momentum. This is a once-in-a-lifetime opportunity, and you must constantly ask yourself, "Am I making the most out of this situation?" You want to constantly evaluate and reevaluate your own performance at your internship: "Am I doing the very best I can? What else can I do?" In my experience, this is the difference between an average intern and a stand-out intern. The sections below provide tips to help you stand out. I titled each heading with what the employer should be saying about you (the intern).

## "They are always the first to volunteer!"

We know to volunteer for everything. But do you actually follow that rule? At your internship, one student will be the first to volunteer. Make sure that individual is you. This is a quick and easy way to show that you take initiative and don't rely on others to get things done. It also shows that you don't mind doing the less glamorous tasks. If you are interning at an interior design firm and want to sit in on a client meeting—that's super normal. Everyone wants to sit in on a client meeting. However, if you volunteer to set up the meeting space or make copies of the materials the client needs (tasks that aren't the coolest), that's what will stand out to the employer.

## "They are always alert!"

When the employer calls your name, you should give your undivided attention. Unless you are preoccupied with another assignment, you should go right over to him or her, look alive, friendly, attentive, and even excited—and have a pen and paper with you. To show your dedication, take notes on everything the employer says. Never roll your eyes or look frustrated when an employer asks you to do a task.

## "I've never seen them just sitting around."

Find work for yourself. The second you complete a task or have nothing to do, get out of your seat and ask the internship coordinator if he or she needs anything. If that person doesn't need anything, ask who else in the department needs help. I mentioned this earlier in the networking section. If no one has work for you, read anything you can get your hands on. Every industry has a variety of trade publications associated with it. For example, in publishing, you should be reading *Publishers Weekly* every week, and you should also sign up for daily industry news emails such as *PWDaily*, *Shelf Awareness*, and *Publishers Lunch*. Take advantage of the resources at your company and build your knowledge of the news and events taking place in your industry of choice.

## "When I give them tasks, they take me seriously."

Any time an employer assigns you work, you take notes, listen to everything he or she has to say, and then ask questions. Take pride in your work and go the extra mile to let the employer know this is a priority for you and something you take very seriously.

## "I trust them."

Trust is a big issue at an internship. As an intern, you handle paperwork and overhear confidential matters. You won't always be told what is private and what is public information. Just to be safe, keep all of the company information private. Don't gossip to friends or family about who that company represents, badmouth any clients, or talk about financial information. Every company has some sort of sensitive information associated with it. Keep everything you hear or learn in-house. Once the people in an organization feel they cannot trust you, they will let you go from your internship. Keep in mind that trust isn't always associated with confidential information or paperwork—it applies to all of your actions.

## "They know what they've accomplished."

Write out what you've accomplished. Keep track of all of the tasks that you've done during your internship. If you communicate with your boss through emails, checking *sent* emails is a great way to do this. Make a quick list of the majority of tasks you've accomplished and next to each, write down the learning objective. In chapter 5, we discussed how every task has a learning objective tied to it. As an example, let's take a look at my task list from my newspaper internship:

1. **Fact-checking for special issues.** Learning Objective(s): cold-calling, communicating with different types of people, the importance of printing accurate information, learning how frequently information

changes, how to stay organized when putting in several outgoing calls, phone etiquette

2. **Proofreading.** Learning Objective(s): editing experience, strategies for editing, what editors look for during the proofreading process, the value of a proofreader to a writer

3. **Managing contributor deadlines.** Learning Objective(s): networking with writers/contributors, the importance of deadlines, communicating with unique personalities

4. **Writing for publication.** Learning Objective(s): helping develop writing style, providing constant feedback from editorial team, publishing for one of the first times

5. **Assisting production team.** Learning Objective(s): understanding value of entire team working together, watching the process from the producer's and designer's perspectives, communicating one part of a project to another team involved in the process, relationship management in the workplace, how an entire newspaper is put together on a weekly basis

Going through and actually writing out the learning objectives will help you understand the full benefit of the opportunity. As the internship goes on, you tend to forget the real value of what you're doing.

# PROBLEMS AT YOUR INTERNSHIP

Although you do not plan for problems at your internship, you must prepare for them. Whenever you work with new people and are placed in a unique environment, conflicts may occur. Here are some of the most common internship issues and how to appropriately deal with them.

## Missing Days of Your Internship

Before your internship starts, look at your calendar. Are you going on any trips? Is your family taking a vacation? Do you have a wedding, graduation, or another event you cannot miss? Mark those dates down on your calendar. Tell the internship coordinator as soon as you get offered the position that you are available the entire summer from X date to X date with the exception of whichever dates you need to miss. If you need to miss more than three days, it might be worth having a phone conversation with the employer. I suggest offering to make up the internship hours on another day or week. This shows that you take the internship seriously and honor the commitment. You should think hard before agreeing to any last-minute trips or romantic getaways. Your internship commitment is a big one, and you should try to miss the least amount of days possible.

If you are sick and need to miss a day of your internship, call the internship coordinator as soon as you know he or she is in the office. Leave a message or tell the coordinator over the phone what the problem is, apologize, and say you will make up the hours. If you know the coordinator prefers to communicate by email, go ahead and write a sincere note. Your internship coordinator would rather you stay home than bring your illness to the office. Just don't make a habit of calling in sick. If something happens and you must miss several days, have a phone conversation with your internship coordinator ahead of time so they are aware of your situation.

## Burning Bridges

Understanding how to properly network is mandatory at an internship. You cannot afford to harm relationships with potential employers. I placed a student at an engineering company last summer. He reported directly to the head of the firm. Every Friday the head of the company would bring in students and meet with them about current projects. This process made the students feel very important to the company. They all looked forward to Fridays.

One of his fellow interns, Robert, seemed to be favored by the internship coordinator (a different person in the office). All of the interns watched him get constant invites into business meetings—something the rest of them never got. These invitations were highly coveted at the company. None of the interns understood why he was picked over the rest of them. They were jealous. Some of the interns (thank goodness, it was not the student I placed) decided to exclude Robert from the group. They didn't invite him to sit with them at lunch or to gatherings after work. They started a rumor that he'd purchased his way into the company. Robert eventually heard what everyone was whispering about and told his father about it. The following day, the head of the engineering company told the interns he was extremely disappointed with some them and how we were treating one another. It turns out Robert was his son. He cancelled the remainder of their Friday meetings. Remember, everyone knows everyone. You must have that mentality at your internship.

## Changing Your Internship Hours

If your work schedule changes or another commitment comes up and you must change your internship hours, ask your internship coordinator if you can schedule a time to talk about it. This can be over the phone or in person. Before you get on that call, have an idea of what you specifically want your new hours to be. The less the amount of work you leave for the employer to figure out, the easier the conversation will be. Being prepared means always having a solution available.

## Ending Your Internship Early

An internship is a commitment—a big commitment. There is really no excuse for ending it early. Of course, if an emergency situation arises, you can ask to schedule a time to speak with your internship coordinator and be as honest as possible about the situation. Decide how you want the conversation to end before you get on the phone. The employer needs to know if you can no longer do the internship or if you just need to cut back on hours. Make your end goal come across throughout the conversation so you don't confuse the employer or make the employer feel like you are wasting his or her time. Make sure that you value and prioritize your commitments. Leaving an internship early can harm relationships with potential employers. Even if employers say they aren't bothered by this, normally they are. If they put time and effort into your internship, they want to get the time and effort back from you.

# Problems with Coworkers or Fellow Interns

Because this is an internship and not a full-time job, you only need to deal with your coworkers and fellow interns for a brief period of eight to fifteen weeks. Unless you feel uncomfortable or threatened by a coworker or fellow intern, consider this a challenge. In life, you will work with people of all shapes, sizes, colors, and personalities. We become stronger individuals by learning to work with others who have different opinions and perspectives. Bite your tongue to the best of your ability in this situation. Use this as a life lesson in working with others. Most importantly, don't let their negative energy affect your mood and don't gossip about them.

# If You Aren't Happy at Your Internship

I had fifteen internships in college. Each came with their individual upsides and downsides. More importantly, each provided a thorough look at different career choices and helped me learn more about myself and how I wanted to spend my time after college. While at an internship, don't concentrate on whether that company is your dream job; concentrate on learning all you can. Like I said at the beginning of this chapter, focus on how you can make the most of the opportunity.

# ♛ INTERN QUEEN CHAPTER ESSENTIALS

- Make sure you introduce yourself to as many people at your internship as possible. Remember to give your first and last name.
- Understand what it means to create deeper relationships with professional contacts.
- Develop a system in the office and at home for organizing your contacts.
- Identify executives at your internship or outside of your internship that you potentially want to meet, research their information, and reach out to approximately twenty people to set informational

meetings. Remember to come up with a list of questions ahead of time.

- Read over my internship tips to help you score big points at your internship.
- Review the information on how to deal with problems at your internship so you are prepared to handle anything that comes your way.

We've reached the end of another chapter. You've worked so hard to get this internship position. Don't let it slip out of your fingers! Grab control of your situation, your future—and run with it. Now that you know how to perform, network, stand out, and avoid conflict at your internship, we can discuss how to turn these internships into job opportunities.

I started this chapter with the story of how I reached out to Ken Baker. Just to reinforce how powerful one contact can be, I want to point to the same example. As mentioned, Ken Baker eventually left *Us Weekly* and went on to work for E! I launched internqueen.com in 2009 and asked Ken if he could do anything to help me get the word out. Within seconds of my call, he put internqueen.com on the homepage of the E! website. Everyone is a professional contact, and you never know what someone's next gig will be. Always stay in touch.

## CHAPTER 9

# After the
# **Internship**

*One day,* during one of the *coolest* internships I had, working with high profile celebrities, magazines, and designers, I was called into my boss's office and asked to shut the door behind me. He told me that one of the assistants in his department was leaving. Did I want a job? The moment felt surreal. Was this really happening? I remember a surge of energy passing through my body and envisioning myself walking celebrities down red carpets, attending photo shoots, and making appearances at glamorous parties.

And then I snapped out of it. Unfortunately the reality of the situation was that I was moving to Orlando that fall to start my junior year at University of Central Florida. The only glamorous job I'd be doing was attending class and waiting tables at the Improv Comedy Club—not exactly the life of an A-list publicist. Sadly I told my boss I couldn't accept the position. I knew in the bigger picture, school was my top priority (for the moment).

Looking back, that was the only internship that directly led to a job offer. Did that mean my other internships weren't worth it? Of course not! In fact, the professional contacts I built at my internships are still paying off on a daily basis. While an internship does not guarantee a job with an employer, it does guarantee an experience—an experience that takes you one step closer to where you want to be after college.

It's commonplace for large employers and corporations to use their internship programs as recruitment tools. As I mentioned in chapter 6, *Bloomberg Businessweek* identifies the top 50 internship programs. The majority of these employers recruit a large percentage of their summer interns for entry-level hires. Employers topping that list year after year include PricewaterhouseCoopers, Proctor & Gamble, KPMG, and Disney. Let's take a look at some statistics from the *Bloomberg Businessweek* list from 2009 (the most recent year the document was published).[1]

Ernst & Young:
Number of Interns in 2009: 1,971
Percentage of Interns That Received Job Offers: 92%

General Electric:
Number of Interns in 2009: 3,060
Percentage of Interns That Received Job Offers: 40%

Proctor & Gamble:
Number of Interns in 2009: 496
Percentage of Interns That Received Job Offers: 83%

Target:
Number of Interns in 2009: 911
Percentage of Interns That Received Job Offers: 71%

These impressive stats prove that internships can lead directly to employment. I encourage you to read over the full list of employers mentioned. You can find them on businessweek.com by searching the word *internships* and scrolling through their "Best of . . ." lists.

But whether your internship leads directly to employment or not, you need to be thinking of what comes after your internship. In this chapter, I'll discuss how to prepare for the end of your internship, the best ways to stay in touch with your professional contacts, and how to begin the job search. If you leave your internship and don't stay connected, you will miss out on opportunities. By the end of this chapter, you will feel confident in your ability to turn any internship into a potential job.

# TWO WEEKS BEFORE YOUR INTERNSHIP ENDS

As your internship comes to an end, do not get senioritis. This is actually one of the most crucial parts of the entire process. Two weeks before your final day, I want you to do the following: ask the employer for a letter of recommendation, update your resume, evaluate what you want, and purchase and write thank-you notes. Let's look a little closer at each of these.

## Ask the Employer for a Letter of Recommendation

Employers are busy, and even if you are their favorite intern, it may take them a week or so to generate a letter for you. Ask them two weeks before the end of the internship. That gives you enough time to ask them once and then remind them one week later. The best way to ask employers for a letter of recommendation is by using their favorite means of communication. How does your employer communicate with you the most regularly? Skype? Text? Phone? Email? In person? Use whatever communication method you think the employer prefers. Asking for a recommendation is a normal and common request, so do not feel intimidated. When I needed a letter of recommendation from my internship coordinator at FOX, I emailed her:

Hi Sarah,

I can't believe my internship comes to an end in two weeks! I wanted to ask you for a letter of recommendation before the end of my internship. I know you are super busy, so I wanted to make sure I asked ahead of time. I really appreciate your continuous support and guidance throughout this amazing opportunity.

Best,
Lauren Berger

Reference the lists you've been keeping updated on the tasks you've accomplished while at your internship. This is going to help you update your resume in the step below.

## Update Your Resume!

It's best to complete this task before you forget. While you are at your internship, you are still in work mode. Many students leave and go into play mode after their internship and never get around to updating their resume. Add your most recent experience to the top of your resume. When describing your position, use the information from the task list. Skim your task list. Highlight the skills you've developed and the results you've achieved that you feel are most beneficial and will help you at your next position. Select four to briefly highlight as you describe your internship on your resume; you can use either sentences or bullet points.

## Evaluate What You Want

Two weeks before the end of your internship, take a few days to think long and hard about what you want your next step to be. Are you graduating or in a position where you could accept a job with the company? Are you interning at a company with high turnover that could potentially have a job opening? Do you want to connect with professionals you know your boss knows? Do you want to meet anyone that your boss is friendly with? Think about your next step and ask your internship coordinator if you can set up a meeting with him or her. If your internship coordinator is not your boss, you may also suggest a lunch or grabbing coffee for a few minutes over the next two weeks to discuss your future. An email requesting such a meeting would read something like this:

Hi Sarah,

Our time together is coming to an end! I cannot believe how this internship has flown by. I wanted to reach out and see if we could get together to grab coffee at some point over the next two weeks. I'd love to hear more about how you got started and get advice.

Please let me know when you might be available.

Best,
Lauren Berger

## Purchase and Write Thank-You Notes

We spoke about handwritten thank-you notes when we discussed interviews in chapter 5. You need these notes at the end of your internship as well. Purchase your thank-you notes at least two weeks before the end of your internship so you can start writing them and have them ready to be mailed the last day of your internship. Thank-you cards to internship coordinators, employers, and other contacts can stay short. Here's an example:

Sarah,

I wanted to thank you so much for an amazing summer internship at FOX. The tasks I learned, relationshipo I built, and goals I accomplished are priceless, and I will carry the lessons learned at FOX for life. I can't believe how much I learned about the television world, script coverage, and what goes into making a new show. Thank you for always taking the extra time to make sure I understood each assignment and constantly providing helpful feedback. Please stay in touch.

Sincerely,
Lauren Berger

As mentioned in chapter 8, everyone on your contact list (that you are keeping in Excel) should receive a thank-you card. Individually mail the notes to each person; never hand out thank-you cards or put them on an executive's desk.

# HOW TO STAY IN TOUCH

My rule for staying in touch with employers is simple: touch base once per semester. I'm no longer in school, yet I still follow this rule and reach out to my professional contacts once in the fall, spring, and summer. Normally I'll reach out after Labor Day to say hello and ask my contacts how their summer went and if they went on any interesting trips. After the new year (spring), I'll check in and see how their holidays went, and in June, I'll wish them a great summer and an amazing summer internship season (something that's obviously unique to my position at internqueen.com). Other great times to reach out are holidays and birthdays. Try and get your employer's birth date and add it to your calendar as a yearly occurrence. Don't flat out ask your employer for his or her birthday. Be discrete!

I reach out to my contacts three times per year because I'm building and maintaining real, deeper relationships as we discussed in the previous chapter. You don't want to only reach out to someone when you *need* something. The goal is to constantly ask yourself, "What can I bring to the table?" Let's walk through an example. One of the executives I worked under at BWR (actually the one who offered me the job years ago) is still at BWR. A few years back he was named a vice president at the company. I emailed him as soon as I heard about his promotion to say, "Congratulations!" Take any opportunity like this to stay in touch with a contact. Since I reached out when he received his promotion, I didn't reach out the rest of the semester. You don't want to bombard anyone. I keep in touch with this executive three times per year (as I've explained), so this year when I emailed him to check in and say hello, he wrote back that he was looking for an assistant. He asked if I knew anyone. One of my best friends happens to be an outstanding assistant, so I immediately sent over her resume and put her at the top of his wish list for an assistant. Always think about where you can add value—even if the opportunity doesn't present itself that directly or clearly.

Think about what information was valuable to that person while you interned under them. For example, my old boss at CAA had a baby when I left. To this day, whenever I see a cute little boy's clothing store, I'll send her a short note and tell her to check it out and provide the address. Ken Baker and I have a friend in common. One of my closest friends was his publicist at E! a few years back. Whenever I'm with that friend, I'll drop Ken a note that we both say hello. If you intern for a production company or a talent agency that's always looking for great comedy writers and comedians, and a few months after your internship you happen to be at a comedy club and spot an amazing up-and-coming talent, share that information! These are just a few examples of how to bring value to the table. You want to get in the habit of developing these two-way relationships so you don't end up with an abundance of one-sided relationships. I work with certain people who only email me when they need things, and, after a while, I notice. It makes me no longer want to help them. Build a two-way relationship that benefits both parties. You will come to appreciate the support network, and one day when you really need advice or a favor, you will be thankful you stayed in touch.

# STAY CONNECTED

Once you leave an internship, stay connected. Don't throw an entire summer of work experience out the window. Let's say you had an internship at a social media firm. Each week you were responsible for covering different clients and watching over specific accounts. The next time you read an article or hear something about one of those clients, send a link over to your old internship coordinator and say, "This is great!" or "Congrats!" You can also set your Google Alerts (google.com) to notify you anytime a client is named in a news article. This can keep you in the loop and help you bring valuable information to your old contacts.

As I mentioned before, you must be cautious of having any professional communication over social networks. After your internship, it is not appropriate to friend your internship coordinator or employer on Facebook unless they initiate it or you have formed a friendship with them outside of the office. If you have set up your LinkedIn profile, it is appropriate to add them to your network, as this site tends to be used more for professional networking than for personal social networking. You should already be following the company you interned for on Twitter and Facebook and I encourage you to stay engaged and connected by commenting and liking things frequently.

# YOU ARE READY TO WORK— NOW WHAT?

You graduate from college. Everyone celebrates. The one looming question is—where will you work? Will you be able to land a job? The process of getting a job after college changes depending on the industry and the specific employer. For example, many finance or business students will get job offers immediately following a summer internship for the following year. Normally these come in formal offer letters in the mail or over email. I want to focus our attention on the jobs for which you don't receive offer letters months before you graduate.

You may find yourself in the situation where you have to seek out a job as opposed to having an employer seek you out to offer you a job. If the job you want is in an industry centered in a particular city or region of the country, odds are you will have to live in the city where the employer is located before they take your application seriously. Let's break the following notes down into steps. We'll call this "what to do once you graduate."

## Step 1: Live Where You Want to Work

Don't be afraid. Want to live in Texas? Move to Texas. Want to live in San Diego? Move to San Diego. You don't have to land your dream job instantly. If you work part-time for a retail or restaurant chain, you might be able to transfer to another franchise in the city you'd like to live in. If not, pick up a part-time job as soon as you arrive to finance your life while you take your time and find the job that is best suited for you.

I didn't call my contact in Los Angeles about wanting job interviews until I lived in Los Angeles. The majority of these companies want you to start *yesterday*. This may sound frustrating. You might be thinking, "Well, what if it doesn't work out? I don't want to move somewhere unless I have a job opportunity first." And that's a fair thought. Unfortunately that's the way most businesses work. The good thing about this form of instant hiring is that it forces you to make a firm decision about your future. Want to live and work in New York City? Get to New York City. And don't call us until you do. As I've mentioned in previous sections of this book, employers want to see your confidence. The second they sense hesitation, they don't want to hire you. Why should they hire someone in Florida who *might* be moving to New York? What if you aren't serious? Doesn't it make more sense to interview someone who already lives in New York?

## Step 2: Get Back in Touch with Professional Contacts

Two months before you graduate, I suggest reaching out to all of your professional contacts. If you've already graduated, that's fine, go ahead and reach out now. Concentrate on the contacts you have in the area where you want to live. For example, I was going to school in Florida, but I wanted to live in Los Angeles. Right before I graduated, I started emailing my contacts in Los Angeles and asking them if I could set up calls to get advice about my plans for postgraduation. My million-dollar question for them on the calls was this: "I'm about to graduate in two months. I know that I want to live in Los Angeles and work in the entertainment industry. What do you suggest I do until I move out to Los Angeles and once I arrive there?" The most common answer I got was "Call me when you get here." Professionals do not take you as seriously until you actually live where you say you want to live. Remember the old saying? Talk is cheap.

## Step 3: Tap into Their Personal and Professional Networks

Once you physically move to the location where you want to work, your goal is to reconnect with all of your contacts who offered to help you once you're in the area. You want to find a way to connect with anyone they know who might be hiring. Here are some questions to ask when reconnecting.

- Whom do you suggest I connect with to find out about potential job opportunities?
- What professional associations should I try to join to meet new people and hear about any job openings?
- Are there any specific people that you think I should reach out to and try to connect with?
- What resources do you suggest I follow and track to monitor new job opportunities?

Again, you ask these questions because the ultimate goal is for your professional contact to put you in touch with their professional contacts.

# Step 4: Create Your Daily Job-Search Plan

When I moved to Los Angeles from Florida, I felt an instant rush of excitement and a bit of anxiety. I knew my savings would last a few months, but I wanted to find a job as soon as possible. I also didn't want to settle on just any job. I wanted to be picky and land a position I was truly excited about that would teach me the ropes of Hollywood. I put together a job plan similar to the one I describe below. People in any industry can follow a job plan like this while starting their job search.

| THE DAILY JOB-SEARCH PLAN | |
|---|---|
| 8:00 a.m. | Wake up, do your morning rituals, look over trade publications specific to the industry in which you are interested. *TIP: If you had an·internship in that industry, ask former internship coordinators what trade publications you should be reading daily and weekly. They might even share their online username and password with you!* |
| 9:30 a.m. | Scan relevant job sites and put any interesting positions into Excel document. |
| 11:00 a.m. | Change the scenery. Sometimes changing locations helps refresh your brain. I like to bounce back and forth between my place and the local coffee shops. Scope out places with free WiFi in your neighborhood. Time for follow-ups and more outreach to set general meetings with contacts or executives you might have even when a job opportunity is not available. These meetings help remind people that you are job hunting and are a good time for you to pick their brains and tap into their personal and professional networks. |
| 3:00 p.m. | Finished for the day. Go play! |

- Look at your calendar and mark down the date that is two weeks before your final day.
- Ask your employer for a letter of recommendation two weeks before your last day.
- Set aside time to write down all of the tasks you completed. Make a list of learning objectives that coincide with each task.
- Update your resume. Always keep it current.
- Block out some time to evaluate your internship and really think about what you want your next step to be. Schedule a meeting with your internship coordinator to discuss your options.
- Take out those thank-you cards again. Do you have enough left? Go purchase more, if necessary.
- Save all of your new contacts' information wherever you've elected to store this information. I suggest using an email client (not your college email server) such as Gmail or Outlook.
- Put reminders in your calendar for June 1, September 1, and February 1 to reach out to your professional contacts.
- Determine how you will stay connected to your internship. What industry-related blogs will you follow, trade publications will you read, and so on?
- If you will graduate from college this semester or have already graduated, create your daily job-search plan.

Read through this information, absorb this information, and please follow my advice. If your internship doesn't directly lead to a job—it's okay. Use the ways I'm teaching you to network and get the most out of your relationships to land a job on your own terms. No matter where you are in your current internship hunt (beginning or end), it's vital that you understand the bigger picture and how you can leverage your experience and turn it into a career. I'm looking forward to watching each one of you do big things and rise to the top of our generation.

# EPILOGUE

WHEN I SAT DOWN MONTHS AGO to write this book, I thought, "How did I get to where I am today? When did I change from a college student who only cared about parties and football games to someone dedicated and passionate about building their future?" It was at that first internship at the Zimmerman Agency. I spoke about that transformational period in chapter 1, and I want to reiterate that you can *all* have your click moment. I will be lucky if I'm the person who encourages you to seek out that opportunity.

When I was a student, no one told me I could run my own business. In fact, most people spent their time telling me what I couldn't do. If I had listened to them, I wouldn't be writing this book today. The only reason I know how to run my business, create and market my brand, get international publicity, and manage a team is because I was lucky enough to intern and work for years under so many successful executives.

As we near the end of our internship journey together, I cannot help my excitement. Internships change lives. And if you've made it all the way through this book, that shows dedication to *your* life. You are in the driver's seat and will control where you end up. It's easy to talk about where you want to be, what you want to do, the places you want to work, and experiences you want to have, but finding a way to actually get there is a constant challenge.

Now that you've finished reading this book, keep it. Reference it at different points throughout your internship, mark off the check lists as you start and finish your internship journey. My hope is that you continuously open this book throughout your college and professional career as so much of the advice is interchangeable.

   I guess this is where we part ways. My goal as the Intern Queen is to provide you with an outlet—a place to chat, vent, complain, ask questions, and learn more about internships and college advice. This isn't good-bye, as I pride myself in being accessible to my audience. I invite you to continue our newfound friendship through my website, Twitter, and Facebook. An internship will change your life, and I cannot wait to hear all about it. Good luck!

# ENDNOTES

## Chapter 1

1. National Association of Colleges and Employers, "2010 Student Survey," http://www.naceweb.org/Research/Student/Student_Survey.aspx ?referral=research&menuID=70&nodetype=4 (conducted April 30, 2010).
2. Mary Mahoney (assistant director of Career Services, University of Tennessee), in discussion with author, May 2011.
3. National Association of Colleges and Employers, "2010 Student Survey," http://www.naceweb.org/Research/Student/Student_Survey.aspx ?referral=research&menuID=70&nodetype=4 (conducted April 30, 2010).
4. Jennifer Rupert (assistant director of Career Services, the New School), in discussion with author, May 2011.
5. Jane Linnenburger (director of Career Center, Bradley University), in discussion with author, May 2011.
6. Elizabeth Saunders (CEO, Real Life E), in discussion with author, May 2011.
7. Gabrielle Bernstein (author of *Spirit Junkie*), in discussion with author, May 2011.

## Chapter 2

1. *Princeton Review*, "Top 10 College Majors," http://www.princetonreview .com/college/top-ten-majors.aspx (accessed May 1, 2010).
2. Beth Shapiro Settje (internship resources manager at the Department of Career Services, University of Connecticut), in discussion with author, May 2011.

## Chapter 3

1. Ross Herosian (manager of College Programs and HR Products, Sirius XM Radio), in discussion with author, May 2011.
2. Alicia Valko, Sample Resume. Reprinted by permission.
3. Andrea Teggart, Sample Cover Letter. Reprinted by permission.

## Chapter 4

1. Dan Schawbel (Author of *Me 2.0: 4 Steps to Building Your Future*), in discussion with author, May 2011.
2. Chandra Robrock (student at Florida State University), in discussion with author, May 2011.
3. Facebook, "Statistics," http://www.facebook.com/press/info.php?statistics (accessed January 3, 2011).
4. Ibid.
5. Julio Guzman, email message to author, May 2011.

## Chapter 5

1. Max Durovic, email message to author, May 2011.
2. Alyssa Allen, email message to author, September 2010.

## Chapter 6

1. US Department of Labor, *Fact Sheet #71: Internship Programs Under the Fair Labor Standards* ACT, http://www.dol.gov/whd/regs/compliance/whdfs71.pdf.
2. *Blog Maverick,* "Want an Unpaid Internship So You Can Get Valuable Experience?—Screw You!" blog entry by Mark Cuban, September 5, 2009.
3. Lindsey Gerdes, "Top Undergrad Internship Programs," *Bloomberg Businessweek,* http://images.businessweek.com/ss/09/12/1210_best_internship_companies/1.htm.
4. US Equal Employment Opportunity Commission, "Sexual Harassment," http://www.eeoc.gov/laws/types/sexual_harassment.cfm.

5. Justine Lisser, (senior attorney-advisor, Office of Communications & Legislative Affairs, Equal Employment Opportunity Commission), in discussion with author, February 2011.
6. Ibid.
7. Ibid.
8. Ibid.

## Chapter 9

1. Lindsey Gerdes, "Top Undergrad Internship Programs," *Bloomberg Businessweek*, http://images.businessweek.com/ss/09/12/1210_best_internship_companies/1.htm.

# ABOUT THE AUTHOR

*Bloomberg Businessweek* magazine named Lauren Berger one of America's Best Young Entrepreneurs 25 and Under in 2009. America Online says, "If you are going to college and wondering what you are going to do this summer—you need to look her up." Mobile Youth has placed her in the top 10 Youth Marketing Minds.

Lauren Berger is CEO of Intern Queen, Inc. and internqueen.com, an online internship destination and lifestyle brand that encourages students to make the most of their college years through internships. Berger grew up in Clearwater, Florida, where her parents still reside. She participated in fifteen internships during her four years of college, hence the title "Intern Queen." Berger earned a degree in organizational business communications at the University of Central Florida and interned across the country for top-notch companies such as MTV, FOX, BWR Public Relations, and NBC.

Now, as CEO of Intern Queen, Inc. and an international speaker, Berger works with over one thousand employers located all over the globe. Her site, internqueen.com, reaches hundreds of thousands of students, parents, and employers each month. She has connected students worldwide with the internships of their dreams. Berger speaks at high schools, colleges, and young professional groups across the country. She has been featured in the *New York Times, Wall Street Journal, Washington Post,* TeenVogue .com, MarieClaire.com, and EOnline.com, and has appeared on *CBS Sunday Morning* and local morning shows across the country. Lauren lives in Toluca Lake, California. To contact Lauren or read her blog, please visit www.internqueen.com.

# INDEX

importance of, 7
after internships, 174–76
*See also* Contacts
New York City, 144–45, 150

P
Packing
  for internships, 151–53
  for interviews, 112–14
Parking, 136
Part-time jobs, 18
Passports, 149
Perma-interns, 10
Personal branding, 65, 66–77
Phone
  etiquette, 143
  interviews by, 88–89
Pop accessories, 108, 111
Portfolios, 61–62, 112, 115
Posture, 114
Preparation
  importance of, 122–23, 154
  for interviews, 97–105
Problems, dealing with, 164–67
Purses, 112

Q
Questions
  asking, during internship,
    132, 142
  for interviews, 100–105
Quid pro quo, 128, 130–31

R
Receptionists, talking with,
  33–34, 114
Recommendation, letters of, 56,
  58–60, 171–72
References
  character, 58
  on resumes, 48
  turning contacts into, 8–9
Rejection, dealing with, 1–2
Relationships
  starting, 131
  types of, 157–58
Restaurant interviews, 93–94,
  109–10
Resumes
  bringing, to interviews, 113
  building experience for, 8
  checklist for, 48–51
  color and, 48–49
  consistency of, 49
  contact information section of,
    44–46
  content of, 50
  education section of, 46–47
  emailing, 43
  example of, 52
  font for, 49
  length of, 49
  on LinkedIn, 75–76
  objective on, 49–50
  photos on, 49
  previous experience section of, 47
  references section of, 48
  relevancy test for, 50–51

# NOTES

# MORE CAREER GUIDANCE FROM TEN SPEED PRESS

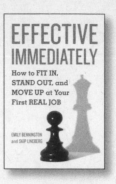

**What Color Is Your Parachute?** 2012
*A Practical Manual for Job-Hunters and
Career-Changers*
by Richard N. Bolles
$18.99 paperback (Canada: $20.00)
ISBN: 978-1-60774-010-0
eBook ISBN: 978-1-60774-076-6

**Effective Immediately**
*How to Fit In, Stand Out, and Move Up
at Your First Real Job*
by Emily Bennington and Skip Lineberg
$14.99 paperback (Canada: $18.99)
ISBN: 978-1-58008-999-9
eBook ISBN: 978-1-58008-421-5

**Resume 101**
*A Student and Recent Grad Guide to
Crafting Resumes and Cover Letters
that Land Jobs*
by Quentin J. Schultze
$12.99 paperback (Canada: $14.99)
ISBN: 978-1-60774-194-7
eBook ISBN: 978-1-60774-195-4
ON SALE MARCH 6, 2012

**10 Things Employers Want You
to Learn in College**
*The Know-How You Need to Succeed*
by Bill Coplin
$14.99 paperback (Canada: $18.99)
ISBN: 978-1-58008-524-3

Available from Ten Speed Press wherever books are sold.
**www.tenspeed.com**